# Bertie's Year

*12 Fast-and-Easy Quilts
from a Little Wool and Flannel*

Bonnie Sullivan of All Through the Night

# Dedication

*To the memory of Grandpa Bert and Grandma Ruby.*
*Many of my fondest childhood memories were*
*made spending time with them on their farm.*

Bertie's Year: 12 Fast-and-Easy Quilts
from a Little Wool and Flannel
Copyright© 2020 by Bonnie Sullivan

This book was produced and published
by All Through the Night, LLC,
Salem, Oregon 97302
www.AllThroughTheNight.net

Publisher: All Through the Night, LLC
Appliqué Design: Bonnie Sullivan
Graphic Designer: Angie Haupert Hoogensen
Illustrator: Sandy Loi
Photographers: Adam Albright, Brent Kane

Photography for this book was taken at the
homes of Tracie Fish of Kenmore, Washington,
and Libby Warnken of Ankeny, Iowa.

For questions or concerns
regarding editorial content, contact
All Through the Night, LLC at
www.AllThroughTheNight.net.

DISTRIBUTOR
To order copies of this book for
wholesale, retail, or individual
sale, contact:

Martingale
18939 120th Ave. NE, Suite 101
Bothell, WA 98011-9511 USA
ShopMartingale.com

ISBN: 978-1-68356-110-1

Printed in Hong Kong
25 24 23 22 21 20      8 7 6 5 4 3 2 1

# Contents

# Introduction

Welcome to a year in the life of Bertie, my favorite little brown bird. I had such a great time dreaming up scenes for Bertie to explore throughout the year—my hope is that you will enjoy them too.

Bertie is named for my grandfather, Bert. He loved the outdoors and was an amazing gardener who could grow anything, including some of the best corn on the cob and the biggest juiciest raspberries. Grandpa would pick a fresh juicy peach from one of his trees, warm from the sun, and cut it up for us to eat. And it was always a special treat when he was harvesting honey and would give us each a piece of honeycomb filled with sweet, sticky honey to chew on.

He and my grandma Ruby had a 40-acre farm and raised cows, pigs, and chickens. I remember the big hay fields that we played in (he probably wasn't too happy about that) and orchard of filbert trees we would hide in. A smaller garden by the house was filled with all sorts of fruits and vegetables, and my grandma had a flower cutting garden right beyond the clothesline. The February design reminds me of Bert and Ruby.

Originally I designed each Bertie scenario as a small wall hanging to celebrate a month of the year and the changing seasons so that you could take one down and put up the next in the same spot. But I knew some quilters would rather turn their year of Bertie blocks into one big quilt. So for added inspiration, starting on page 59 you'll find a materials list for sashing and borders as well as assembly instructions for two different quilt layouts.

Whether you make just one or two Bertie designs or you go all in and make a large quilt, I hope you have just as much fun stitching Bertie throughout the year as I did.

~ *Bonnie*

# Easy Wool Appliqué

*My knowledge of working with wool has come in bits and pieces over the years. What you'll find here are the methods that work well for me.*

## finding and felting wool

When I started working with wool, it wasn't readily available at quilt shops or from online vendors. I searched through secondhand stores for 100% wool clothing that I could cut apart and felt to use for appliqué. Once I became a vendor at International Quilt Market (a wholesale trade show), I found fabulous hand-dyed wool and then fell even deeper in love with wool. Hand-dyed wool offers rich, subtle color variations, and as a bonus, it has already been felted so it's ready to use.

In addition to using hand-dyed wool for some of the pieces in *Bertie's Year,* I also like using "as-is" wool, which is just as it says—you use the wool just as it comes off the bolt. Today we have so many choices of plaids, tweeds, herringbones, and more. We call these *textures,* and they work nicely with hand-dyed wool, giving you the opportunity to have subtle variations in color and texture in each appliqué block or project.

You can find hand-dyed and as-is wool at many quilt shops. If your local shop doesn't carry wool, two of my favorite sources are Blackberry Primitives (BlackberryPrimitives.com) and Mary Flanagan Woolens (MFWoolens.com). Check them out, but don't limit your choices—you'll find many sources for wool by doing a quick online search.

If you're buying wool right off the bolt, you'll need to felt it before using. I felt wool by washing it in hot water, rinsing it in cold water, and then drying it in a hot dryer. Don't overdry it or you could end up with set-in creases. Damp dry is good; you can then hang it to finish drying completely before using or storing the wool. When you felt the wool, the fibers become matted together, reducing the chance of unraveling along the edges.

## cutting out appliqués

One of the things I like most about wool appliqué is that you don't have to turn under the edges. Generally, wool doesn't have a right and wrong side. However, look at each piece closely; you may find that you prefer one side over the other. Whichever side you like best can be the right side.

For *Bertie's Year,* I used fusible appliqué. When you use fusible web, you iron it to the wrong side of the fabric, which means the right side will be the reverse image of the shape you trace. That's why all the patterns in this book have already been reversed, with birds and other shapes facing in the opposite direction of the finished appliqués. When you use fusible web, your shapes will end up looking just like they do in the photographs.

However, if you prefer *not* to use fusible web, you can prepare appliqué templates from freezer paper. One advantage of this method is that you can save the templates and reuse them. With fusible web, the shapes will adhere to the wool, and therefore they aren't reusable. Let's have a look at both methods so you can choose the one you like best.

## freezer paper

As mentioned above, you can reuse freezer-paper shapes a number of times. When a pattern calls for cutting five leaves, you can cut one freezer-paper shape and use that one template for each leaf.

1 Trace the shapes onto the uncoated side of the freezer paper.

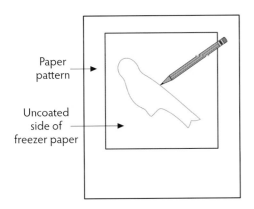

Paper pattern

Uncoated side of freezer paper

2 Roughly cut out each shape.

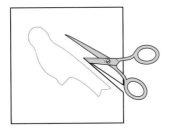

3 Iron the shiny side of the freezer paper to the *wrong* side of the wool you want to use. (Be sure to iron to the wrong side because the shapes have been reversed from the finished piece.) Cut out the shapes on the drawn lines and peel the paper before appliquéing the pieces to the background fabric.

Wrong side of wool

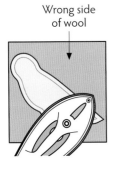 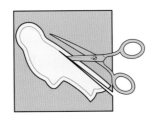

## fusible web

I used the fusible-web method for the projects in this book. While I've tried a variety of brands over the years, my favorite is Shades SoftFuse. It's very lightweight, pliable, easy to sew through, and it doesn't gum up my needle. Remember, when you use fusible web, the finished design will be the reverse of the shapes you've traced. The patterns in this book have already been reversed for you, so simply trace them and your finished design will match the projects shown.

1 Trace the shapes onto the paper side of the fusible web. Roughly cut around the outside of each shape.

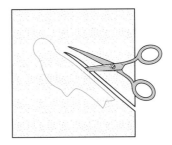

2 Iron the glue (bumpy) side of the fusible to the wrong side of the wool, following the manufacturer's instructions. Let the fusible web cool and then cut out the shapes on the drawn lines. Remove the paper backing.

Paper side of fusible web

Wrong side of wool

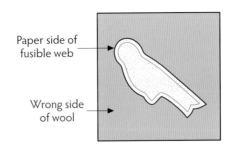

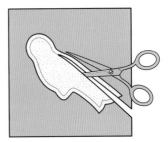

**3** With an iron, press the pieces in place on the right side of the background fabric, using plenty of heat to penetrate the wool. Once the pieces are adhered, turn the fabric over and press from the wrong side of the background flannel to give the adhesive the best chance of fusing the layers together.

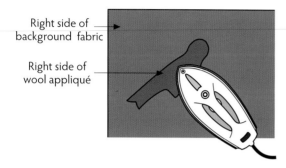

Right side of background fabric

Right side of wool appliqué

## stitching the pieces

Whether you've used freezer paper or fusible web, you'll need to stitch the appliqués to the background to secure them permanently. I prefer to use a whipstitch. While a blanket stitch is frequently used for wool appliqué, I like how the whipstitch seems to disappear. It's much less noticeable than the blanket stitch, and it works particularly well for small pieces.

When it comes to whipstitching, I use any type of thread that blends with my wool—regular sewing thread, quilting thread, or a single strand of embroidery floss. I'm not particular about the type of thread, but I do want it to match the color of the wool. Make your stitches about ⅛" long and about ⅛" apart for an even look. The stitches should be perpendicular to the edge of the appliqué piece, as shown in the photo below.

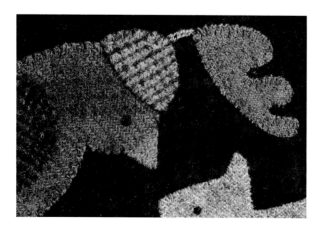

# Embroidery Stitches

All the decorative stitching in *Bertie's Year* is done with size 12 Valdani pearl cotton. I've used only a handful of colors throughout the book. To replicate the look of my projects, you'll need the following colors:

- P1 Old Brick (red)
- P2 Olive Green (green)
- P4 Aged White (white)
- P5 Tarnished Gold (gold)
- O178 Tea-Dyed Stone (gray)
- O513 Coffee Roast (dark brown)
- 1 Black Dyed

Of course, you can substitute your favorite brand or use three strands of embroidery floss if you prefer.

Following are the basic stitches I frequently use. A few of the months include a less well-known stitch, and those are illustrated with that month's instructions.

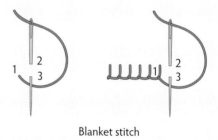

Blanket stitch

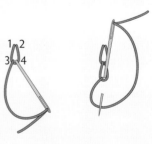

Chain stitch

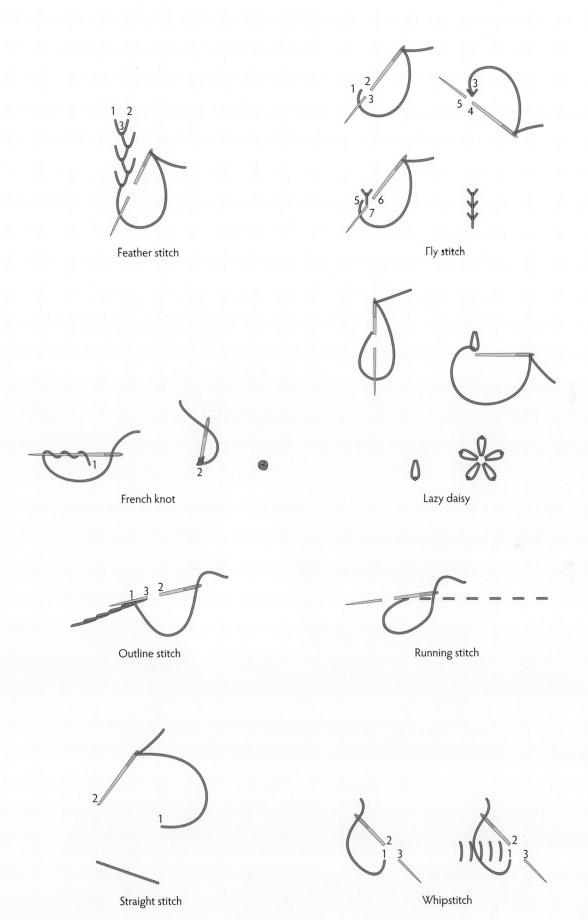

Feather stitch

Fly stitch

French knot

Lazy daisy

Outline stitch

Running stitch

Straight stitch

Whipstitch

# January

*Bertie makes sure to don a red woolen cap before venturing out on a limb to visit Mr. Snowman on a chilly winter day.*

■ FINISHED SIZE: 13" × 17"

# materials

*This project was made using Woolies flannels from Maywood Studio with wool appliqué.*

½ yard of espresso houndstooth (black) flannel for background, borders, and backing

2 squares, 3" × 3" *each*, of 6 assorted red flannels for patchwork border (12 squares total)

5" × 10" piece of brown wool for branches

3" × 9" piece of green wool for holly leaves

4" × 5" piece of off-white wool for snowman

1" × 1" square of orange wool for carrot nose

3" × 7" piece of light brown wool for bird

2" × 4" piece of medium brown herringbone, tweed, or plaid wool for bird's wing

2" × 3" piece of red wool for hat

1" × 1" square of gold wool for beak

13½" × 17½" piece of lightweight batting

9 red buttons (⅜" to ½" diameter) for holly berries

Sewing thread or embroidery floss in colors to match wool-appliqué pieces

Size 12 Valdani pearl cotton for embroidery details:
- O513 Coffee Roast
- O178 Tea-Dyed Stone
- P1 Old Brick
- P2 Olive Green
- P5 Tarnished Gold
- 1 Black Dyed
- P4 Aged White

Fusible web

# cutting

**From the black flannel, refer to the cutting guide below to cut:**
- 2 pieces, 9¼" × 13½"
- 1 piece, 9" × 13"
- 2 strips, 1" × 16½"
- 2 strips, 1" × 13½"
- 12 squares, 3" × 3"

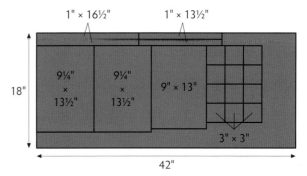

Cutting guide for black flannel

# preparing appliqué pieces

Trace the appliqué patterns (page 65) onto fusible web. The pieces are already reversed so you can trace directly on the paper backing of the fusible web. Loosely cut around the traced shapes. Iron the fusible shapes onto the *wrong* side of the wool (choose the side you like best for the right side) in the colors indicated on the pattern pieces. Then cut out the pieces on the traced lines.

# appliquéing the design

1 Arrange the appliqués on the black flannel 9" × 13" piece. The background will be trimmed to 8½" × 12½" after the appliqué is complete, so be sure to keep the shapes within these dimensions. The left end of the branch should end ¼" from the edge of the flannel. Tuck some pieces under others as indicated on the assembly diagram on page 13. When satisfied with the placement, fuse all the pieces in place.

2 Whipstitch the pieces to the background using matching thread. Try to keep the stitches about ⅛" apart and ⅛" deep into the appliqués. Keep the stitches perpendicular to the edges of the shapes.

3. Referring to "Embroidery Stitches" on page 8 as needed, use pearl cotton to add embroidery details:

- Using Olive Green, outline stitch the veins and stems of the leaves.

- Using Old Brick, outline stitch the tie for the hat.

- Using Tarnished Gold, make a double row of outline stitches for the bird's leg and a single row of outline stitches for the foot.

- Using Black Dyed, make French knots for the bird's eye, snowman's eyes, and snowman's buttons.

- Using Coffee Roast, make three rows of outline stitches for the snowman's twig arm and one row of outline stitches for the fingers.

## adding the border

1. Press the design and trim the appliquéd center to 8½" × 12½", trimming evenly all around the piece.

2. Draw a diagonal line from corner to corner on the wrong side of the red flannel 3" squares. Pair each red square with a black flannel square, right sides together. Stitch ¼" from each side of the drawn lines and then cut apart on the drawn lines to make 24 half-square-triangle units. Press the seam allowances open and trim the units to 2½" square.

Sew ¼" from both sides of the drawn line.

Cut apart on the drawn line.

Press seam allowances open and trim blocks to 2½".

3. Referring to the assembly diagram on page 13, make four patchwork borders using six half-square-triangle units each. The numbers in the diagram refer to the six different red flannels to help you mix them up for a scrappy border.

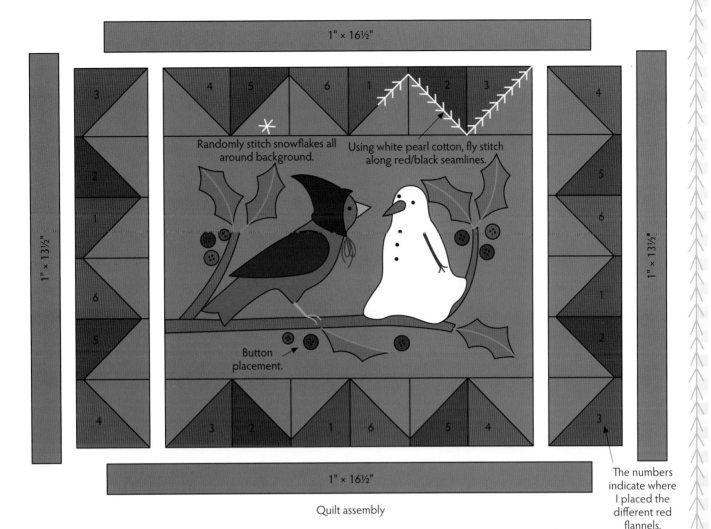

1" × 16½"

1" × 13½"

Randomly stitch snowflakes all around background.

Using white pearl cotton, fly stitch along red/black seamlines.

Button placement.

1" × 13½"

1" × 16½"

The numbers indicate where I placed the different red flannels.

Quilt assembly

4 Sew the top and bottom border to the appliquéd center, then add the side borders. Press. Stay stitch around the perimeter, about ⅛" from the edges.

5 Using Aged White pearl cotton, fly stitch along the seamlines between the red and black triangles and make straight stitches to add snowflakes randomly in the black background area.

6 Using black sewing thread, stitch the nine red buttons to the design for holly berries.

# finishing

To complete the project as shown, refer to "Finishing Techniques" on page 58. You will need the black flannel 1" × 13½" and 1" × 16½" strips as well as the two black flannel 9¼" × 13½" rectangles.

Alternately, if you prefer to join the 12 appliqué pieces into one large quilt, turn to "All Year with Bertie" on page 59 for sashing and border cutting instructions and assembly directions for two quilt options.

# February

*Dainty bleeding hearts beautifully frame a romantic pair of lovebirds. Love is in the air!*

■ FINISHED SIZE: 13" × 17"

# materials

*This project was made using Woolies flannels from Maywood Studio with wool appliqué.*

½ yard of espresso houndstooth (black) flannel for background, borders, and backing

2 squares, 3" × 3" *each*, of 5 assorted green flannels for patchwork border (10 squares total)

5" × 7" piece of light brown wool for birds

3" × 4" piece of medium brown herringbone, tweed, or plaid wool for birds' wings

5" × 9" piece of green wool for grassy mound and leaves

2" × 3" piece of gray wool for top hat

1" × 1½" piece of gray houndstooth wool for hatband

1" × 1½" piece of gold wool for birds' beaks

2" × 4" piece of pink wool for bleeding hearts

1" × 1½" of off-white wool for bleeding hearts

13½" × 17½" piece of lightweight batting

1 small white button (¼" or ⅜" diameter) for top hat

Sewing thread or embroidery floss in colors to match wool-appliqué pieces

Size 12 Valdani pearl cotton for embroidery details:
- P2 Olive Green
- P5 Tarnished Gold
- P4 Aged White
- 1 Black Dyed

Fusible web

Pink colored pencil (optional)

# cutting

**From the black flannel, refer to the cutting guide below to cut:**
- 2 pieces, 9¼" × 13½"
- 1 piece, 9" × 13"
- 2 strips, 1" × 16½"
- 2 strips, 1" × 13½"
- 10 squares, 3" × 3"
- 4 squares, 2½" × 2½"

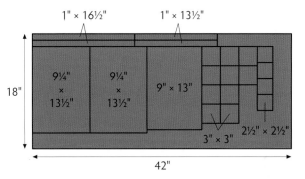

Cutting guide for black flannel

# preparing appliqué pieces

Trace the appliqué patterns (pages 66 and 67) onto fusible web. The pieces are already reversed so you can trace directly on the paper backing of the fusible web. Loosely cut around the traced shapes. Iron the fusible shapes onto the *wrong* side of the wool (choose the side you like best for the right side) in the colors indicated on the pattern pieces. Then cut out the pieces on the traced lines.

# appliquéing the design

1 Arrange the appliqués on the black flannel 9" × 13" piece. The background will be trimmed to 8½" × 12½" after the appliqué is complete, so be sure to keep the shapes within these dimensions. The bottom edge of the grassy mound should be placed ¼" from the edge of the flannel. Tuck some pieces under others as indicated on the assembly diagram on page 17. When satisfied with the placement, fuse all the pieces in place.

2 Whipstitch the pieces in place using matching thread. (You can use sewing thread, quilting thread, or a single strand of floss). Try to keep the stitches about ⅛" apart and ⅛" deep into the appliqués. Keep the stitches perpendicular to the edges of the shapes.

3 Referring to "Embroidery Stitches" on page 8 as needed, use pearl cotton to add embroidery details:

- Using Olive Green, outline stitch the stem of the bleeding hearts and the stems and veins of the leaves.

- Using Tarnished Gold, make a double row of outline stitches for the birds' legs and a single row of outline stitches for their feet.

- Using Black Dyed, outline stitch the definition line on the female bird's face. Make French knots for the birds' eyes.

- If desired, use a pink colored pencil to add blush to the female bird's cheek.

## adding the border

1 Press the design and trim the appliquéd center to 8½" × 12½", trimming evenly all around the piece.

2 Draw a diagonal line from corner to corner on the wrong side of the green flannel 3" squares. Pair each green square with a black flannel square, right sides together. Stitch ¼" from each side of the drawn lines and then cut apart on the drawn lines to make 20 half-square-triangle units. Press the seam allowances open and trim the units to 2½" square.

Sew ¼" from both sides of the drawn line.

Cut apart on the drawn line.

Press seam allowances open and trim blocks to 2½".

3 Referring to the assembly diagram on page 17, make two patchwork borders, each with six half-square-triangle units. Repeat to make two borders each with four half-square-triangle units. The numbers in the diagram refer to the five different green flannels to help you mix them up for a scrappy border.

4 Sew the longer borders to the top and bottom of the appliquéd center. Sew a black flannel 2½" square to each end of the remaining borders and then sew them to the sides of the appliquéd center. Press. Stay stitch around the perimeter, about ⅛" from the edges.

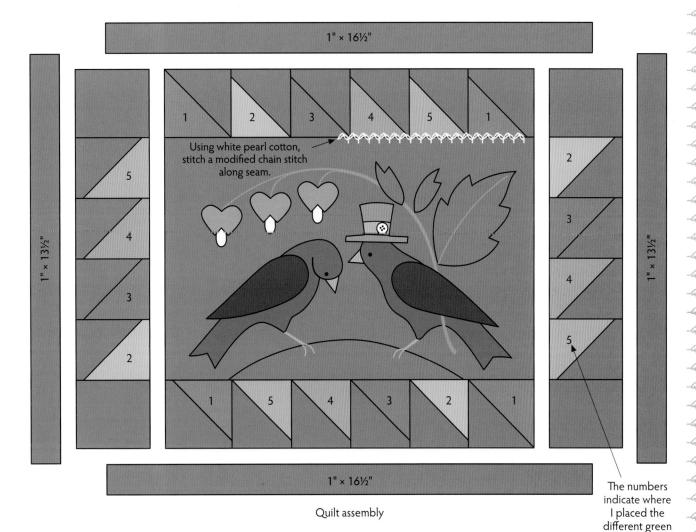

Using white pearl cotton, stitch a modified chain stitch along seam.

The numbers indicate where I placed the different green flannels.

1" × 16½"

1" × 13½"

1" × 13½"

1" × 16½"

Quilt assembly

5   Using Aged White pearl cotton, stitch a modified chain stitch along the seam of the pieced border. Make a lazy daisy stitch at an angle over the seamline. Make another lazy daisy stitch starting in the open end of the previous stitch. On every other daisy stitch make the tacking stitch longer, as shown.

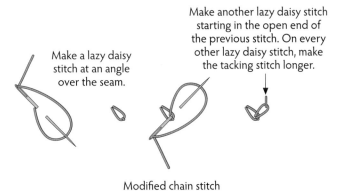

Make a lazy daisy stitch at an angle over the seam.

Make another lazy daisy stitch starting in the open end of the previous stitch. On every other lazy daisy stitch, make the tacking stitch longer.

Modified chain stitch

6   Using off-white sewing thread, sew the small white button to the hatband.

## finishing

To complete the project as shown, refer to "Finishing Techniques" on page 58. You will need the black flannel 1" × 13½" and 1" × 16½" strips as well as the two black flannel 9¼" × 13½" rectangles.

Alternately, if you prefer to join the 12 appliqué pieces into one large quilt, turn to "All Year with Bertie" on page 59 for sashing and border cutting instructions and assembly directions for two quilt options.

# March

*Bertie welcomes the start of spring with a nod to our pollinating friends, the bees. Wearing a bumblebee cap is a must for those blustery March days.*

■ FINISHED SIZE: 13" × 17"

## materials

*This project was made using Woolies flannels from Maywood Studio with wool appliqué.*

½ yard of espresso houndstooth (black) flannel for background, borders, and backing

3 squares, 3" × 3" *each*, of 4 assorted gold flannels for patchwork border (12 squares total)

3" × 7" piece of light brown wool for bird

2" × 4" piece of medium brown herringbone, tweed, or plaid wool for bird's wing

4" × 4" square of gold-and-black plaid wool for bee skep

2" × 2" square of yellow wool for hat and bee

1" × 2" piece of black wool for stripe on hat

1" × 1" square of gold wool for beak

6" × 8" piece of green wool for shamrocks

13½" × 17½" piece of lightweight batting

1 small white button (¼" or ⅜" diameter) for hat closure

Sewing thread or embroidery floss in colors to match wool-appliqué pieces

Size 12 Valdani pearl cotton for embroidery details:
- P2 Olive Green
- P5 Tarnished Gold
- O178 Tea-Dyed Stone
- 1 Black Dyed

Fusible web

## cutting

**From the black flannel, refer to the cutting guide below to cut:**
- 2 pieces, 9¼" × 13½"
- 1 piece, 9" × 13"
- 2 strips, 1" × 16½"
- 2 strips, 1" × 13½"
- 12 squares, 3" × 3"

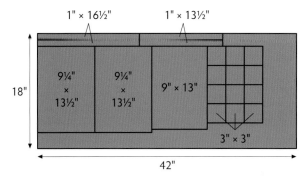

Cutting guide for black flannel

## preparing appliqué pieces

Trace the appliqué patterns (page 68) onto fusible web. The pieces are already reversed so you can trace directly on the paper backing of the fusible web. Loosely cut around the traced shapes. Iron the fusible shapes onto the wrong side of the wool (choose the side you like best for the right side) in the colors indicated on the pattern pieces. Then cut out the pieces on the traced lines.

## appliquéing the design

1 Arrange the appliqués on the black flannel 9" × 13" piece. The background will be trimmed to 8½" × 12½" after the appliqué is complete, so be sure to keep the shapes within these dimensions. Tuck some pieces under others as indicated on the assembly diagram on page 21. When satisfied with the placement, fuse all the pieces in place.

2 Whipstitch the pieces in place using matching thread. Try to keep the stitches about ⅛" apart and ⅛" deep into the appliqués. Keep the stitches perpendicular to the edges of the shapes.

3 Referring to "Embroidery Stitches" on page 8 as needed, use pearl cotton to add embroidery details:

- Using Olive Green, stitch a double row of outline stitches for the shamrock stems.

- Using Tarnished Gold, make a double row of outline stitches for the bird's leg and a single row of outline stitches for the foot. Outline stitch around the hat so that there is more definition between the black stripe and the black background.

- Using Tea-Dyed Stone, use an outline stitch to make two antennae on the hat, finishing each one with a French knot. For the bee's wings, make four lazy daisy stitches. Use a short straight stitch to create the bee's antennae and stinger.

- Using Black Dyed, outline stitch three rows for each stripe on the bee. Make a French knot for the bird's eye. To give more definition to the bee skep, you can add two rows of running stitches as indicated on the appliqué pattern.

## adding the border

1 Press the design and trim the appliquéd center to 8½" × 12½", trimming evenly all around the piece.

2 Draw a diagonal line from corner to corner on the wrong side of the gold flannel 3" squares. Pair each gold square with a black flannel square, right sides together. Stitch ¼" from each side of the drawn lines and then cut apart on the drawn lines to make 24 half-square-triangle units. Press the seam allowances open and trim the units to 2½" square.

Sew ¼" from both sides of the drawn line.

Cut apart on the drawn line.

Press seam allowances open and trim blocks to 2½".

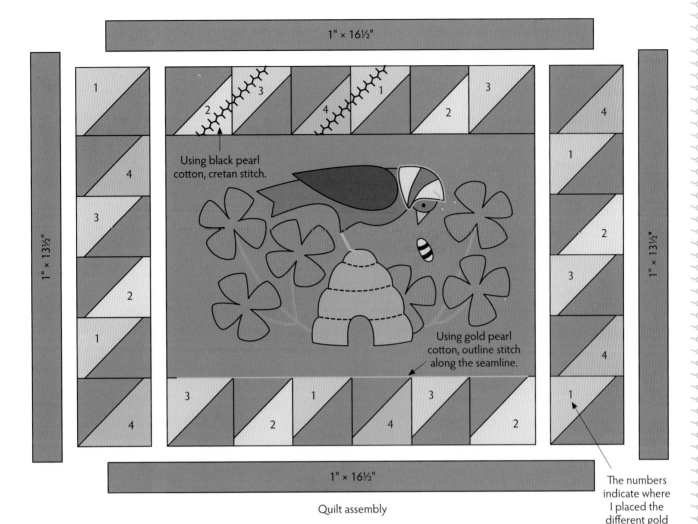

Using black pearl cotton, cretan stitch.

Using gold pearl cotton, outline stitch along the seamline.

1" × 16½"

1" × 13½"

1" × 13½"

1" × 16½"

The numbers indicate where I placed the different gold flannels.

Quilt assembly

3 Referring to the assembly diagram above, make four patchwork borders, each with six half-square-triangle units, noting the orientation of the gold and black triangles. The numbers in the diagram refer to the four different gold flannels to help you mix them up for a scrappy border.

4 Sew borders to the top and bottom of the appliquéd center first, then sew the remaining borders to the quilt sides. Press the seam allowances toward the appliquéd quilt center. Stay stitch around the perimeter, about ⅛" from the edges.

5 Using Tarnished Gold pearl cotton, outline stitch along the seamline of the border and appliquéd center. Use Black Dyed pearl cotton and a Cretan stitch to embroider through the center of each gold strip in the border.

6 Using black thread, sew the small white button to the hat for its closure.

## finishing

To complete the project as shown, refer to "Finishing Techniques" on page 58. You will need the black flannel 1" × 13½" and 1" × 16½" strips as well as the two black flannel 9¼" × 13½" rectangles.

Alternately, if you prefer to join the 12 appliqué pieces into one large quilt, turn to "All Year with Bertie" on page 59 for sashing and border cutting instructions and assembly directions for two quilt options.

# April

*Is that the Easter bunny? Why, no! It's Bertie in a rabbit-eared hat, admiring colorfully decorated eggs in the nest.*

## materials

*This project was made using Woolies flannels from Maywood Studio with wool appliqué.*

½ yard of espresso houndstooth (black) flannel for background, borders, and backing

3 squares, 3" × 3" *each*, of 2 different blue flannels for patchwork border (6 squares total)

2 squares, 3" × 3" *each*, and 2 squares, 2½" × 2½" *each*, of 2 different blue flannels for patchwork border (4 squares total of each size)

3" × 7" piece of light brown wool for bird

2" × 4" piece of medium brown herringbone, tweed, or plaid wool for bird's wing

3" × 5" piece of golden brown wool for nest

5" × 10" piece of brown wool for branches

5" × 6" piece of green wool for leaves

2" × 4" piece of off-white wool for bunny hat

2" × 2" square of pink wool for pink egg

2" × 3" piece of light blue wool for blue eggs

1" × 1½" piece of purple wool for stripe on pink egg

1" × 1" square of gold wool for beak

13½" × 17½" piece of lightweight batting

1 small white button (¼" or ⅜" diameter) for hat closure

Sewing thread or embroidery floss in colors to match wool-appliqué pieces

Size 12 Valdani pearl cotton for embroidery details:
■ P2 Olive Green
■ P5 Tarnished Gold
■ P4 Aged White
■ 1 Black Dyed

Fusible web

## cutting

**From the black flannel, refer to the cutting guide below to cut:**
■ 2 pieces, 9¼" × 13½"
■ 1 piece, 9" × 13"
■ 2 strips, 1" × 16½"
■ 2 strips, 1" × 13½"
■ 10 squares, 3" × 3"

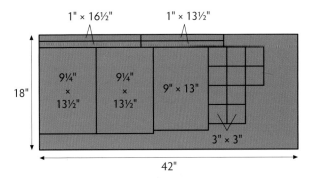

Cutting guide for black flannel

## preparing appliqué pieces

Trace the appliqué patterns (page 69) onto fusible web. The pieces are already reversed so you can trace directly on the paper backing of the fusible web. Loosely cut around the traced shapes. Iron the fusible shapes onto the *wrong* side of the wool (choose the side you like best for the right side) in the colors indicated on the pattern pieces. Then cut out the pieces on the traced lines.

## appliquéing the design

1 Arrange the appliqués on the black flannel 9" × 13" piece. The background will be trimmed to 8½" × 12½" after the appliqué is complete, so be sure to keep the shapes within these dimensions. The end of the main branch should end ¼" inside the left edge of the black flannel background. Tuck some pieces under others as indicated on the assembly diagram on page 25. When satisfied with the placement, fuse all the pieces in place.

2 Whipstitch the pieces in place using matching thread. Try to keep the stitches about ⅛" apart and ⅛" deep into the appliqués. Keep the stitches perpendicular to the edges of the shapes.

3 Referring to "Embroidery Stitches" on page 8 as needed, use pearl cotton to add embroidery details:

- Using Olive Green, outline stitch the veins and stems of the leaves.

- Using Tarnished Gold, make a double row of outline stitches for the bird's leg and a single row of outline stitches for the foot.

- Using Aged White and a variety of embroidery stitches, decorate the eggs.

- Using Black Dyed, make a French knot for the bird's eye.

## adding the border

1 Press the design and trim the appliquéd center to 8½" × 12½", trimming evenly all around the piece.

2 Draw a diagonal line from corner to corner on the wrong side of the blue flannel 3" squares. Pair each blue square with a black flannel square, right sides together. Stitch ¼" from each side of the drawn lines and then cut apart on the drawn lines to make 20 half-square-triangle units. Press the seam allowances open and trim the units to 2½" square.

Sew ¼" from both sides of the drawn line.

Cut apart on the drawn line.

Press seam allowances open and trim blocks to 2½".

3 Referring to the assembly diagram on page 25, make two patchwork borders, each with six half-square-triangle units. Repeat to make two borders each with four half-square-triangle units. The numbers in the diagram refer to the four different blue flannels to help you mix them up for a scrappy border.

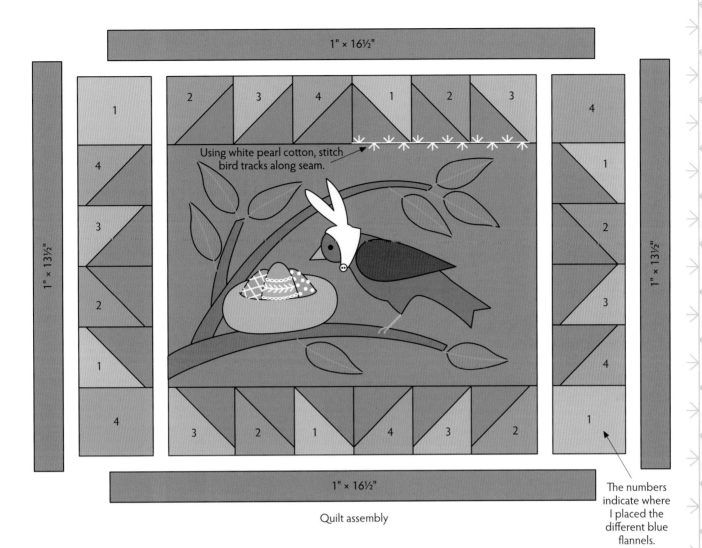

Using white pearl cotton, stitch bird tracks along seam.

1" × 16½"

1" × 13½"

1" × 13½"

1" × 16½"

The numbers indicate where I placed the different blue flannels.

Quilt assembly

4 Sew the longer borders to the top and bottom of the appliquéd center. Sew a blue flannel 2½" square to each end of the remaining borders and then sew them to the sides of the appliquéd center. Press. Stay stitch around the perimeter, about ⅛" from the edges.

5 Using Aged White pearl cotton, stitch bird tracks along the seamline between the appliquéd center and the pieced border. Each bird track is stitched with a series of straight stitches that are about ¼" long. Stitch two horizontal stitches along the seamline. Then add a vertical stitch at their midpoint. Finally, stitch diagonally from the horizontal stitches to make a bird track.

6 Using off-white sewing thread, sew the small white button to the hat for its closure.

## finishing

To complete the project as shown, refer to "Finishing Techniques" on page 58. You will need the black flannel 1" × 13½" and 1" × 16½" strips as well as the two black flannel 9¼" × 13½" rectangles.

Alternately, if you prefer to join the 12 appliqué pieces into one large quilt, turn to "All Year with Bertie" on page 59 for sashing and border cutting instructions and assembly directions for two quilt options.

Bird track stitch

# May

*Who can resist a trip to the flower market in spring? Bertie's loaded a pull-cart basket full of Mother Nature's luscious May flowers.*

## materials

*This project was made using Woolies flannels from Maywood Studio with wool appliqué.*

½ yard of espresso houndstooth (black) flannel for background, borders, and backing

3 squares, 3" × 3" *each*, of 4 assorted blue flannels for patchwork border (12 squares total)

3" × 7" piece of light brown wool for bird

2" × 4" piece of medium brown herringbone, tweed, or plaid wool for bird's wing

4" × 5" piece of golden brown wool for basket and handle

1" × 9" piece of blue wool for basket-pull ribbon

2" × 2" square of gray tweed wool for wheel

2" × 4" piece of pink wool for flowers

2" × 3" piece of yellow wool for flower and bee

2" × 3" piece of purple wool for flowers

3" × 3" square of green wool for leaves and flower bases

1" × 1" square of orange wool for yellow-flower center

1" × 1" square of gold wool for beak

13½" × 17½" piece of lightweight batting

1 black button (¾" diameter) for wheel rim

Sewing thread or embroidery floss in colors to match wool-appliqué pieces

Size 12 Valdani pearl cotton for embroidery details:
- O178 Tea-Dyed Stone
- P2 Olive Green
- P5 Tarnished Gold
- P4 Aged White
- 1 Black Dyed

Fusible web

## cutting

**From the black flannel, refer to the cutting guide below to cut:**
- 2 pieces, 9¼" × 13½"
- 1 piece, 9" × 13"
- 2 strips, 1" × 16½"
- 2 strips, 1" × 13½"
- 12 squares, 3" × 3"

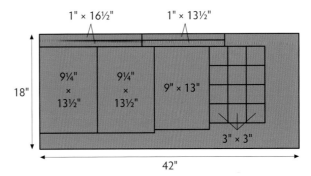

Cutting guide for black flannel

## preparing appliqué pieces

Trace the appliqué patterns (page 70) onto fusible web. The pieces are already reversed so you can trace directly on the paper backing of the fusible web. Loosely cut around the traced shapes. Iron the fusible shapes onto the *wrong* side of the wool (choose the side you like best for the right side) in the colors indicated on the pattern pieces. Then cut out the pieces on the traced lines.

## appliquéing the design

1 Arrange the appliqués on the black flannel 9" × 13" piece. The background will be trimmed to 8½" × 12½" after the appliqué is complete, so be sure to keep the shapes within these dimensions. Tuck some pieces under others as indicated on the assembly diagram on page 29. When satisfied with the placement, fuse all the pieces in place.

2 Whipstitch the pieces in place using matching thread. Try to keep the stitches about ⅛" apart and ⅛" deep into the appliqués. Keep the stitches perpendicular to the edges of the shapes.

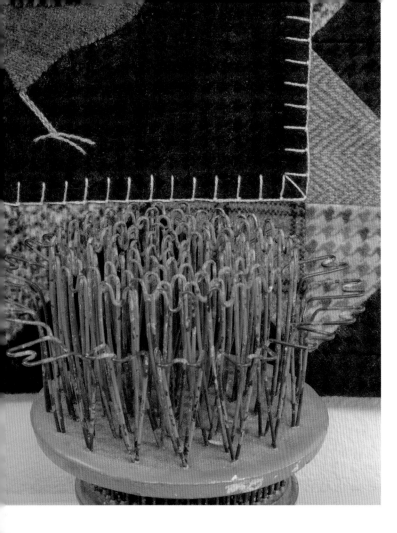

3. Referring to "Embroidery Stitches" on page 8 as needed, use pearl cotton to add embroidery details:

- Using Olive Green, make a double row of outline stitches for the flower stems and the short stem on the blossom hat.

- Using Tarnished Gold, make a double row of outline stitches for the bird's leg and a single row of outline stitches for the foot.

- Using Black Dyed, stitch three rows of outline stitches for each stripe on the bee. Make a French knot for the bird's eye.

- Using Tea-Dyed Stone, make straight stitches for the bee's antennae and stinger. Embroider lazy daisy stitches for the bee's wings.

## adding the border

1. Press the design and trim the appliquéd center to 8½" × 12½", trimming evenly all around the piece.

2. Draw a diagonal line from corner to corner on the wrong side of the blue flannel 3" squares. Pair each blue square with a black flannel square, right sides together. Stitch ¼" from each side of the drawn lines and then cut apart on the drawn lines to make 24 half-square-triangle units. Press the seam allowances open and trim the units to 2½" square.

Sew ¼" from both sides of the drawn line.

Cut apart on the drawn line.

Press seam allowances open and trim blocks to 2½".

3. Referring to the assembly diagram on page 29, make four patchwork borders, each with six half-square-triangle units. The numbers in the diagram refer to the four different blue flannels to help you mix them up for a scrappy border.

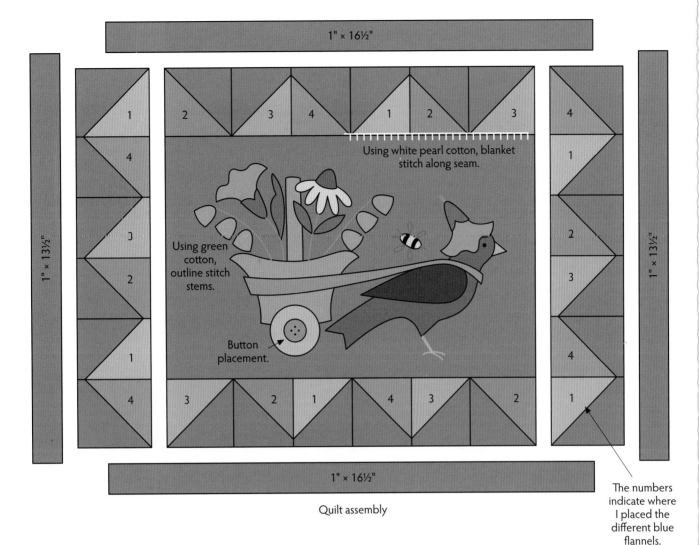

1" × 16½"

1" × 13½"

1" × 13½"

Using white pearl cotton, blanket stitch along seam.

Using green cotton, outline stitch stems.

Button placement.

1" × 16½"

Quilt assembly

The numbers indicate where I placed the different blue flannels.

4 Sew borders to the top and bottom of the appliquéd center first. Then sew the remaining borders to the sides of the appliquéd center. Press. Stay stitch around the perimeter, about ⅛" from the edges.

5 Using Aged White pearl cotton, blanket stitch along the seamline of the pieced border and appliquéd quilt center.

6 Using off-white sewing thread, sew the black button to the center of the wheel.

## finishing

To complete the project as shown, refer to "Finishing Techniques" on page 58. You will need the black flannel 1" × 13½" and 1" × 16½" strips as well as the two black flannel 9¼" × 13½" rectangles.

Alternately, if you prefer to join the 12 appliqué pieces into one large quilt, turn to "All Year with Bertie" on page 59 for sashing and border cutting instructions and assembly directions for two quilt options.

# June

*If it's June, it must be berry season. Bertie is ready to bite into the biggest, juiciest one of the bunch!*

■ FINISHED SIZE: 13" × 17"

# materials

*This project was made using Woolies flannels from Maywood Studio with wool appliqué.*

½ yard of espresso houndstooth (black) flannel for background, borders, and backing

2 squares, 3" × 3" *each*, of 6 assorted green flannels for patchwork border (12 squares total; 2 are extra)

2 squares, 2½" × 2½" *each*, of 2 different green flannels (4 squares total)

3" × 7" piece of light brown wool for bird

2" × 4" piece of medium brown herringbone, tweed, or plaid wool for bird's wing

2" × 6" piece of off-white wool for strawberry blossoms

3" × 4" piece of red wool for ripe strawberries

3" × 3" square of greenish gold wool for unripe strawberries and blossom centers

6" × 6" square of green wool for leaves and strawberry caps

1" × 1" square of gold wool for beak

13½" × 17½" piece of lightweight batting

Sewing thread or embroidery floss in colors to match wool-appliqué pieces

Size 12 Valdani pearl cotton for embroidery details:
- P1 Old Brick
- P2 Olive Green
- P5 Tarnished Gold
- 1 Black Dyed

Fusible web

# cutting

**From the black flannel, refer to the cutting guide below to cut:**
- 2 pieces, 9¼" × 13½"
- 1 piece, 9" × 13"
- 2 strips, 1" × 16½"
- 2 strips, 1" × 13½"
- 10 squares, 3" × 3"

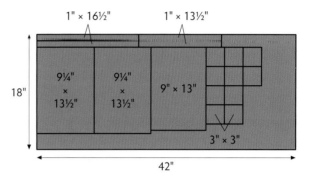

Cutting guide for black flannel

# preparing appliqué pieces

Trace the appliqué patterns (page 71) onto fusible web. The pieces are already reversed so you can trace directly on the paper backing of the fusible web. Loosely cut around the traced shapes. Iron the fusible shapes onto the *wrong* side of the wool (choose the side you like best for the right side) in the colors indicated on the pattern pieces. Then cut out the pieces on the traced lines.

# appliquéing the design

1 Arrange the appliqués on the black flannel 9" × 13" piece. The background will be trimmed to 8½" × 12½" after the appliqué is complete, so be sure to keep the shapes within these dimensions. Tuck some pieces under others as indicated on the assembly diagram on page 33. When satisfied with the placement, fuse all the pieces in place.

2 Whipstitch the pieces to the background using matching thread. Try to keep the stitches about ⅛" apart and ⅛" deep into the appliqués. Keep the stitches perpendicular to the edges of the shapes.

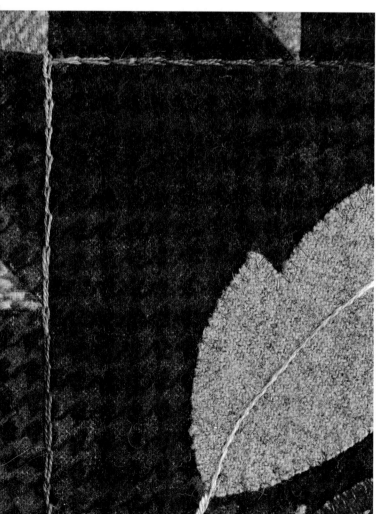

3 Referring to "Embroidery Stitches" on page 8 as needed, use pearl cotton to add embroidery details:

- Using Olive Green, outline stitch the strawberry stems, the tie for the blossom hat, and the veins in the leaves. Make a double row of outline stitches for the main branch.

- Using Tarnished Gold, stitch small straight stitches on the ripe strawberries for their seeds. Make a double row of outline stitches for the bird's leg and make a single row of outline stitches for the foot.

- Using Black Dyed, stitch a French knot for the bird's eye.

## adding the border

1 Press the design and trim the appliquéd center to 8½" × 12½", trimming evenly all around the piece.

2 Draw a diagonal line from corner to corner on the wrong side of the green flannel 3" squares. Pair each green square with a black flannel square, right sides together. Stitch ¼" from each side of the drawn lines and then cut apart on the drawn lines to make 20 half-square-triangle units. Press the seam allowances open and trim the units to 2½" square.

Sew ¼" from both sides of the drawn line.

Cut apart on the drawn line.

Press seam allowances open and trim blocks to 2½".

3 Referring to the assembly diagram on page 33, make two patchwork borders using six half-square-triangle units each and two borders with four half-square-triangle units each. The numbers in the diagram refer to the six different green flannels to help you mix them up for a scrappy border.

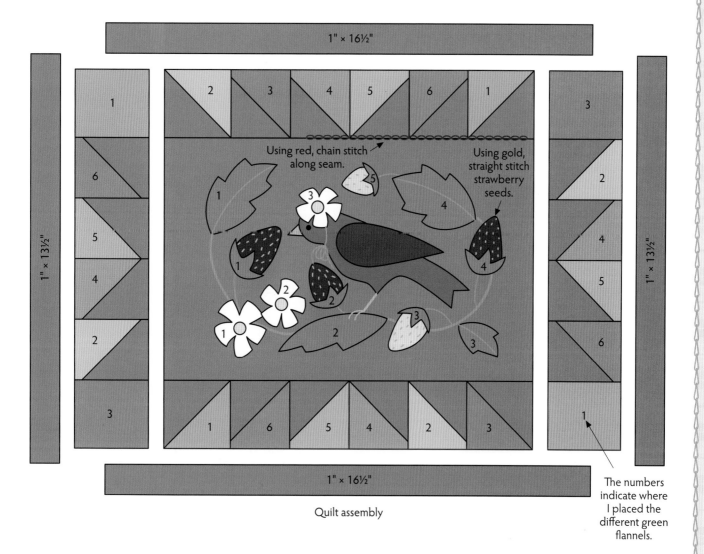

Using red, chain stitch along seam.

Using gold, straight stitch strawberry seeds.

1" × 16½"

1" × 16½"

1" × 13½"

1" × 13½"

Quilt assembly

The numbers indicate where I placed the different green flannels.

4 Sew the top and bottom border to the appliquéd center. Sew a green flannel 2½" square to each end of the side borders. Then sew these to the sides of the appliquéd center. Press. Stay stitch around the perimeter, about ⅛" from the edges.

5 Using Old Brick pearl cotton, chain stitch along the seamlines between the pieced border and the appliqué background.

## finishing

To complete the project as shown, refer to "Finishing Techniques" on page 58. You will need the black flannel 1" × 13½" and 1" × 16½" strips as well as the two black flannel 9¼" × 13½" rectangles.

Alternately, if you prefer to join the 12 appliqué pieces into one large quilt, turn to "All Year with Bertie" on page 59 for sashing and border cutting instructions and assembly directions for two quilt options.

# July

*Like the kid in all of us, Bertie loves a slice of juicy red watermelon—
and he challenges you to a seed-spitting contest.*

■ FINISHED SIZE: 13" × 17"

# materials

*This project was made using Woolies flannels from Maywood Studio with wool appliqué.*

½ yard of espresso houndstooth (black) flannel for background, borders, and backing

2 squares, 3" × 3" *each*, of 5 assorted red flannels for patchwork border (10 squares total)

4" × 7" piece of light brown wool for bird

2" × 4" piece of medium brown herringbone, tweed, or plaid wool for bird's wing

3" × 10" piece of red wool for watermelon

3" × 11" piece of green wool for watermelon rind and leaves

2" × 2" square of blue wool for blueberries

2" × 3" piece of black-and-white plaid wool for hat

1" × 1" square of gold wool for beak

Sewing thread or embroidery floss in colors to match wool-appliqué pieces

Size 12 Valdani pearl cotton for embroidery details:
- P2 Olive Green
- P5 Tarnished Gold
- P4 Aged White
- 1 Black Dyed

Fusible web

# cutting

**From the black flannel, refer to the cutting guide below to cut:**
- 2 pieces, 9¼" × 13½"
- 1 piece, 9" × 13"
- 2 strips, 1" × 16½"
- 2 strips, 1" × 13½"
- 10 squares, 3" × 3"
- 4 squares, 2½" × 2½"

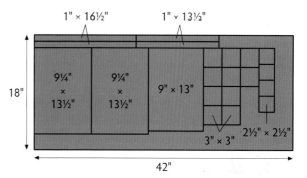

Cutting guide for black flannel

# preparing appliqué pieces

Trace the appliqué patterns (page 72) onto fusible web. The pieces are already reversed so you can trace directly on the paper backing of the fusible web. Loosely cut around the traced shapes. Iron the fusible shapes onto the *wrong* side of the wool (choose the side you like best for the right side) in the colors indicated on the pattern pieces. Then cut out the pieces on the traced lines.

# appliquéing the design

1 Arrange the appliqués on the black flannel 9" × 13" piece. The background will be trimmed to 8½" × 12½" after the appliqué is complete, so be sure to keep the shapes within these dimensions. Tuck some pieces under others as indicated on the assembly diagram on page 37. Note that the watermelon and rind pieces are not overlapped but just butted up to each other. When satisfied with the placement, fuse all the pieces in place.

2 Whipstitch the pieces to the background using coordinating thread. Try to keep the stitches about ⅛" apart and ⅛" deep into the appliqués. Keep the stitches perpendicular to the edges of the shapes.

3 Referring to "Embroidery Stitches" on page 8 as needed, use pearl cotton to add embroidery details:

- Using Olive Green, outline stitch the veins and stems of the leaves. Make a double row of outline stitches for the blueberry stems.

- Using Black Dyed, stitch a French knot for the bird's eye. Stitch a small X on each berry and make lazy daisy stitches for the watermelon seeds. Outline stitch the definition line on the hat.

- Using Aged White, stitch a slightly larger lazy daisy stitch around the black lazy daisy watermelon seeds. Use a running stitch for the path of the spit seed. Fly stitch along the line where the red watermelon meets the green rind.

- Using Tarnished Gold, make a double row of outline stitches for the bird's leg and a single row of outline stitches for the foot.

## adding the border

1 Press the design and trim the appliquéd center to 8½" × 12½", trimming evenly all around the piece.

2 Draw a diagonal line from corner to corner on the wrong side of the red flannel 3" squares. Pair each red square with a black flannel square, right sides together. Stitch ¼" from each side of the drawn lines and then cut apart on the drawn lines to make 20 half-square-triangle units. Press the seam allowances open and trim the units to 2½" square.

Sew ¼" from both sides of the drawn line.

Cut apart on the drawn line.

Press seam allowances open and trim blocks to 2½".

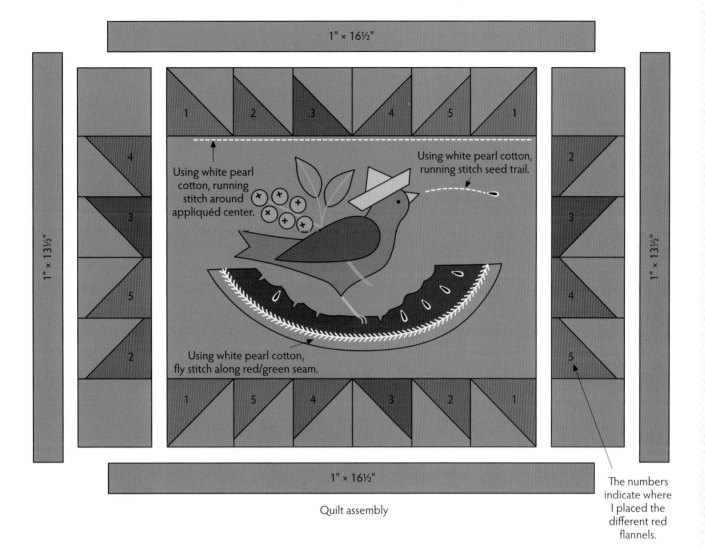

Quilt assembly

The numbers indicate where I placed the different red flannels.

**3** Referring to the assembly diagram above, make two patchwork borders using six half-square-triangle units each and two borders with four half-square-triangle units each. The numbers in the diagram refer to the five different red flannels to help you mix them up for a scrappy border.

**4** Sew the top and bottom borders to the appliquéd center. Sew a black flannel 2½" square to each end of the side borders. Then sew these to the sides of the appliquéd center. Press. Stay stitch around the perimeter, about ⅛" from the edges.

**5** Using Aged White pearl cotton, add a running stitch around the entire appliquéd center, stitching a scant ¼" from the border seamline.

## finishing

To complete the project as shown, refer to "Finishing Techniques" on page 58. You will need the black flannel 1" × 13½" and 1" × 16½" strips as well as the two black flannel 9¼" × 13½" rectangles.

Alternately, if you prefer to join the 12 appliqué pieces into one large quilt, turn to "All Year with Bertie" on page 59 for sashing and border cutting instructions and assembly directions for two quilt options.

# August

*It's worth stepping out to the end of the branch to find the ripest, juiciest pear. Bertie's already enjoying that first bite and sporting a dapper bandana to catch any drips.*

■ FINISHED SIZE: 13" × 17"

## materials

*This project was made using Woolies flannels from Maywood Studio with wool appliqué.*

½ yard of espresso houndstooth (black) flannel for background, borders, and backing

2 squares, 3" × 3" *each*, of 6 assorted red flannels for patchwork border (12 squares total)

3" × 7" piece of light brown wool for bird

2" × 4" piece of medium brown herringbone, tweed, or plaid wool for bird's wing

4" × 10" piece of brown wool for branches

3" × 8" piece of green wool for leaves

3" × 4" piece of light gold wool for pear

1" × 1" square of gold wool for beak

2" × 4" piece of red wool for scarf

1" × 1½" piece of off-white wool for pear bite

13½" × 17½" piece of lightweight batting

Sewing thread or embroidery floss in colors to match wool-appliqué pieces

Size 12 Valdani pearl cotton for embroidery details:
- P2 Olive Green
- P5 Tarnished Gold
- P4 Aged White
- 1 Black Dyed

Fusible web

Pink colored pencil (optional)

## cutting

**From the black flannel, refer to the cutting guide below to cut:**
- 2 pieces, 9¼" × 13½"
- 1 piece, 9" × 13"
- 2 strips, 1" × 16½"
- 2 strips, 1" × 13½"
- 12 squares, 3" × 3"

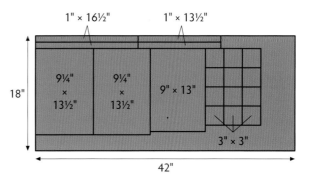

Cutting guide for black flannel

## preparing appliqué pieces

Trace the appliqué patterns (page 73) onto fusible web. The pieces are already reversed so you can trace directly on the paper backing of the fusible web. Loosely cut around the traced shapes. Iron the fusible shapes onto the *wrong* side of the wool (choose the side you like best for the right side) in the colors indicated on the pattern pieces. Then cut out the pieces on the traced lines.

## appliquéing the design

1 Arrange the appliqués on the black flannel 9" × 13" piece. The background will be trimmed to 8½" × 12½" after the appliqué is complete, so be sure to keep the shapes within these dimensions. The ends of the branches should end ¼" inside the right edge of the black flannel. Tuck some pieces under others as indicated on the assembly diagram on page 41. When satisfied with the placement, fuse all the pieces in place.

2 Whipstitch the pieces to the background using matching thread. Try to keep the stitches about ⅛" apart and ⅛" deep into the appliqués. Keep the stitches perpendicular to the edges of the shapes.

3 Referring to "Embroidery Stitches" on page 8 as needed, use pearl cotton to add embroidery details:

- Using Olive Green, outline stitch the veins and stems of the leaves.

- Using Tarnished Gold, make a double row of outline stitches for the bird's leg and a single row of outline stitches for the foot. Make three rows of outline stitches for the pear stem. Stitch a single line of outline stitches for the short definition line at the bottom of the pear.

- Using Black Dyed, stitch a French knot for the bird's eye.

- Using Aged White, stitch French knots on the scarf to make polka dots.

4 If desired, add a little blush to the pear by shading the left and bottom curve with the side of a pink colored pencil.

## adding the border

1 Press the design and trim the appliquéd center to 8½" × 12½", trimming evenly all around the piece.

2 Draw a diagonal line from corner to corner on the wrong side of the red flannel 3" squares. Pair each red square with a black flannel square, right sides together. Stitch ¼" from each side of the drawn lines and then cut apart on the drawn lines to make 24 half-square-triangle units. Press the seam allowances open and trim the units to 2½" square.

Sew ¼" from both sides of the drawn line.   Cut apart on the drawn line.   Press seam allowances open and trim blocks to 2½".

3 Referring to the assembly diagram on page 41, make four patchwork borders using six half-square-triangle units each. The numbers in the diagram refer to the six different red flannels to help you mix them up for a scrappy border.

4 Sew the top and bottom borders to the appliquéd center. Then sew the remaining borders to the sides of the appliquéd center. Press. Stay stitch around the perimeter, about ⅛" from the edges.

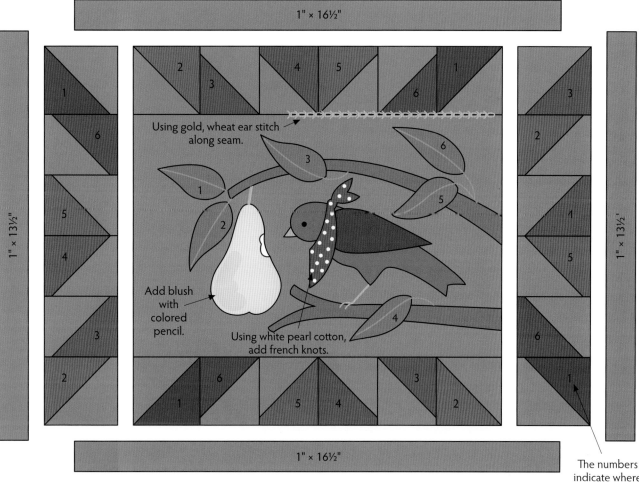

1" × 16½"

1" × 13½"

1" × 13½"

Using gold, wheat ear stitch
along seam.

Add blush
with
colored
pencil.

Using white pearl cotton,
add french knots.

1" × 16½"

The numbers
indicate where
I placed the
different red
flannels.

Quilt assembly

**5** Using Tarnished Gold pearl cotton, add a wheat ear stitch around the entire appliquéd center, stitching along the border seamline.

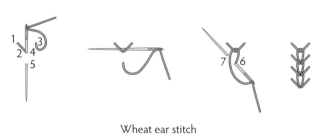

Wheat ear stitch

# finishing

To complete the project as shown, refer to "Finishing Techniques" on page 58. You will need the black flannel 1" × 13½" and 1" × 16½" strips as well as the two black flannel 9¼" × 13½" rectangles.

Alternately, if you prefer to join the 12 appliqué pieces into one large quilt, turn to "All Year with Bertie" on page 59 for sashing and border cutting instructions and assembly directions for two quilt options.

# September

*Mr. Squirrel may be planning to hide all the acorns for the winter, but Bertie is happy to take the acorn caps off his hands. They do make smart-looking fall hats!*

■ FINISHED SIZE: 13" × 17"

## materials

*This project was made using Woolies flannels from Maywood Studio with wool appliqué.*

½ yard of espresso houndstooth (black) flannel for background, borders, and backing

2 squares, 3" × 3" *each*, of 5 assorted green flannels for patchwork border (10 squares total)

4 squares, 2½" × 2½", of green flannel for patchwork border

3" × 7" piece of light brown wool for bird

2" × 4" piece of medium brown herringbone, tweed, or plaid wool for bird's wing

1½" × 13" piece of brown wool for branches

4" × 6" piece of green wool for leaves

2" × 4" piece of golden brown wool for acorns

2" × 3" piece of brown tweed wool for acorn caps

4" × 5" piece of gray wool for squirrel body

3" × 5" piece of gray tweed or plaid wool for squirrel tail

1" × 1" square of gold wool for beak

13½" × 17½" piece of lightweight batting

Sewing thread or embroidery floss in colors to match wool-appliqué pieces

Size 12 Valdani pearl cotton for embroidery details:
■ P2 Olive Green
■ P5 Tarnished Gold
■ 1 Black Dyed

Fusible web

## cutting

**From the black flannel, refer to the cutting guide below to cut:**
■ 2 pieces, 9¼" × 13½"
■ 1 piece, 9" × 13"
■ 2 strips, 1" × 16½"
■ 2 strips, 1" × 13½"
■ 10 squares, 3" × 3"

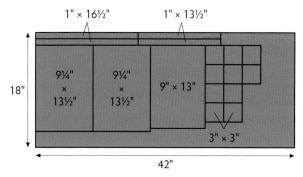

Cutting guide for black flannel

## preparing appliqué pieces

Trace the appliqué patterns (pages 74 and 75) onto fusible web. The pieces are already reversed so you can trace directly on the paper backing of the fusible web. Loosely cut around the traced shapes. Iron the fusible shapes onto the *wrong* side of the wool (choose the side you like best for the right side) in the colors indicated on the pattern pieces. Then cut out the pieces on the traced lines.

## appliquéing the design

1 Arrange the appliqués on the black flannel 9" × 13" piece. The background will be trimmed to 8½" × 12½" after the appliqué is complete, so be sure to keep the shapes within these dimensions. The main branch should end ¼" inside the left and right edges of the black flannel. Tuck some pieces under others as indicated on the assembly diagram on page 45. When satisfied with the placement, fuse all the pieces in place.

2 Whipstitch the pieces to the background using matching thread. Try to keep the stitches about ⅛" apart and ⅛" deep into the appliqués. Keep the stitches perpendicular to the edges of the shapes.

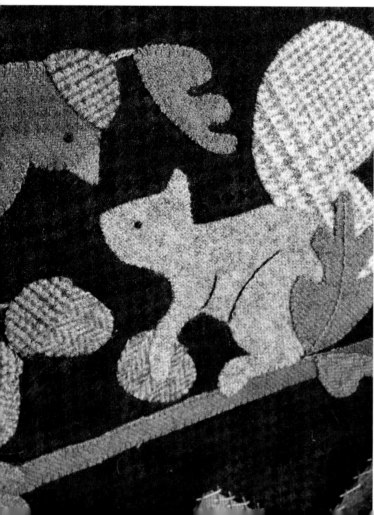

**3** Referring to "Embroidery Stitches" on page 8 as needed, use pearl cotton to add embroidery details:

- Using Olive Green, outline stitch the veins and stems of the leaves. Make a double row of outline stitches for the stems on the acorn caps.

- Using Tarnished Gold, make a double row of outline stitches for the bird's leg and a single row of outline stitches for the foot.

- Using Black Dyed, stitch a French knot for the bird's eye and squirrel's eye. Outline stitch the definition lines on the body of the squirrel.

## adding the border

**1** Press the design and trim the appliquéd center to 8½" × 12½", trimming evenly all around the piece.

**2** Draw a diagonal line from corner to corner on the wrong side of the green flannel 3" squares. Pair each green square with a black flannel square, right sides together. Stitch ¼" from each side of the drawn lines and then cut apart on the drawn lines to make 20 half-square-triangle units. Press the seam allowances open and trim the units to 2½" square.

Sew ¼" from both sides of the drawn line.

Cut apart on the drawn line.

Press seam allowances open and trim blocks to 2½".

**3** Referring to the assembly diagram on page 45, make two patchwork borders using six half-square-triangle units each. Make two borders with four half-square-triangle units each. The numbers in the diagram refer to the five different green flannels to help you mix them up for a scrappy border.

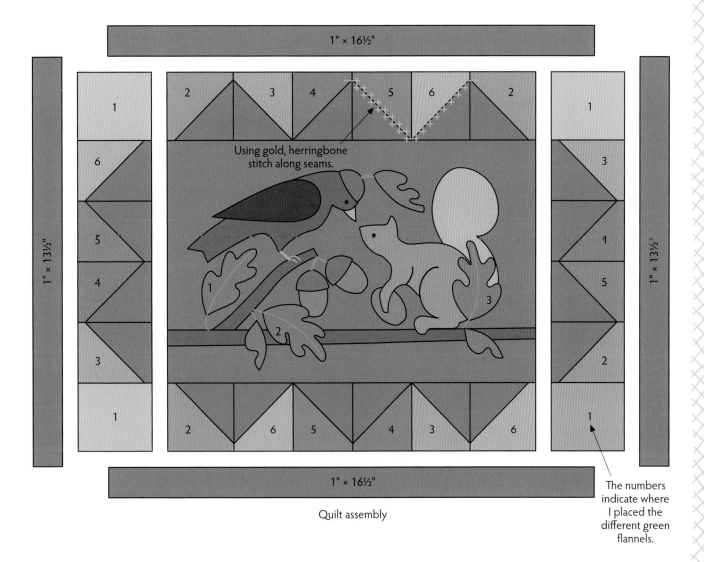

1" × 16½"

1" × 13½"

1" × 13½"

Using gold, herringbone stitch along seams.

1" × 16½"

Quilt assembly

The numbers indicate where I placed the different green flannels.

4 Sew the top and bottom borders to the appliquéd center. Sew a green 2½" square to each end of the shorter borders. Then sew these borders to the sides of the appliquéd center. Press. Stay stitch around the perimeter, about ⅛" from the edges.

5 Using Tarnished Gold pearl cotton, herringbone stitch around the entire appliquéd center, stitching along the seamlines between the green and black flannel.

# finishing

To complete the project as shown, refer to "Finishing Techniques" on page 58. You will need the black flannel 1" × 13½" and 1" × 16½" strips as well as the two black flannel 9¼" × 13½" rectangles.

Alternately, if you prefer to join the 12 appliqué pieces into one large quilt, turn to "All Year with Bertie" on page 59 for sashing and border cutting instructions and assembly directions for two quilt options.

# October

*Boo! This jolly jack-o'-lantern couldn't scare a fly. Or a bird!*
*Bertie welcomes him to the garden while sporting a festive candy-corn hat.*

■ FINISHED SIZE: 13" × 17"

# materials

*This project was made using Woolies flannels from Maywood Studio with wool appliqué.*

½ yard of espresso houndstooth (black) flannel for background, borders, and backing

2 squares, 3" × 3" *each*, of 6 assorted green flannels for patchwork border (12 squares total)

3" × 7" piece of light brown wool for bird

2" × 4" piece of medium brown herringbone, tweed, or plaid wool for bird's wing

3" × 6" piece of green wool for leaves and blossom cap

3" × 7" piece of orange wool for pumpkins and candy corn

2" × 3" piece of yellow wool for pumpkin blossom and candy corn

1" × 2" piece of off-white wool for large pumpkin's eyes and candy corn

1½" × 3" piece of black wool for large pumpkin's mouth

1" × 1" square of red wool for large pumpkin's nose

1" × 1" square of gold wool for beak

2 small black buttons (¼" diameter) for large pumpkin's eyes

13½" × 17½" piece of lightweight batting

Sewing thread or embroidery floss in colors to match wool-appliqué pieces

Size 12 Valdani pearl cotton for embroidery details:
- P1 Old Brick
- P2 Olive Green
- P5 Tarnished Gold
- P4 Aged White
- 1 Black Dyed

Fusible web

White chalk pencil (optional)

# cutting

**From the black flannel, refer to the cutting guide below to cut:**
- 2 pieces, 9¼" × 13½"
- 1 piece, 9" × 13"
- 2 strips, 1" × 16½"
- 2 strips, 1" × 13½"
- 12 squares, 3" × 3"

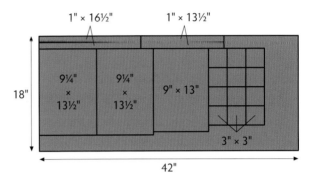

Cutting guide for black flannel

# preparing appliqué pieces

Trace the appliqué patterns (page 76) onto fusible web. The pieces are already reversed so you can trace directly on the paper backing of the fusible web. Loosely cut around the traced shapes. Iron the fusible shapes onto the *wrong* side of the wool (choose the side you like best for the right side) in the colors indicated on the pattern pieces. Then cut out the pieces on the traced lines.

# appliquéing the design

1 Arrange the appliqués on the black flannel 9" × 13" piece. The background will be trimmed to 8½" × 12½" after the appliqué is complete, so be sure to keep the shapes within these dimensions. Tuck some pieces under others as indicated on the assembly diagram on page 49. When satisfied with the placement, fuse all the pieces in place.

2 Whipstitch the pieces to the background using matching thread. Try to keep the stitches about ⅛" apart and ⅛" deep into the appliqués. Keep the stitches perpendicular to the edges of the shapes.

3 Referring to "Embroidery Stitches" on page 8 as needed, use pearl cotton to add embroidery details:

- Using Olive Green, make two rows of outline stitches for the main vine and stem of the small pumpkin. Stitch a single row of outline stitches for the veins and stems of the leaves. For the large pumpkin's stem, make four rows of outline stitches. Note: If you don't want to freehand stitch the tendrils and vine, you can draw them onto the black flannel using a white chalk pencil.

- Using Tarnished Gold, make a double row of outline stitches for the bird's leg and a single row of outline stitches for the foot. Stitch around the petals on the small pumpkin's blossom with a small blanket stitch.

- Using Black Dyed, stitch a French knot for the bird's eye and small pumpkin's eyes. Use outline stitch for the small pumpkin's mouth; use short straight stitches for the mouth ends.

- Using Old Brick, stitch the nose on the small pumpkin using short straight stitches.

- Using Aged White, stitch the black buttons to the whites of the large pumpkin's eyes.

## adding the border

1 Press the design and trim the appliquéd center to 8½" × 12½", trimming evenly all around the piece.

2 Draw a diagonal line from corner to corner on the wrong side of the green flannel 3" squares. Pair each green square with a black flannel square, right sides together. Stitch ¼" from each side of the drawn lines and then cut apart on the drawn lines to make 24 half-square-triangle units. Press the seam allowances open and trim the units to 2½" square.

Sew ¼" from both sides of the drawn line.

Cut apart on the drawn line.

Press seam allowances open and trim blocks to 2½".

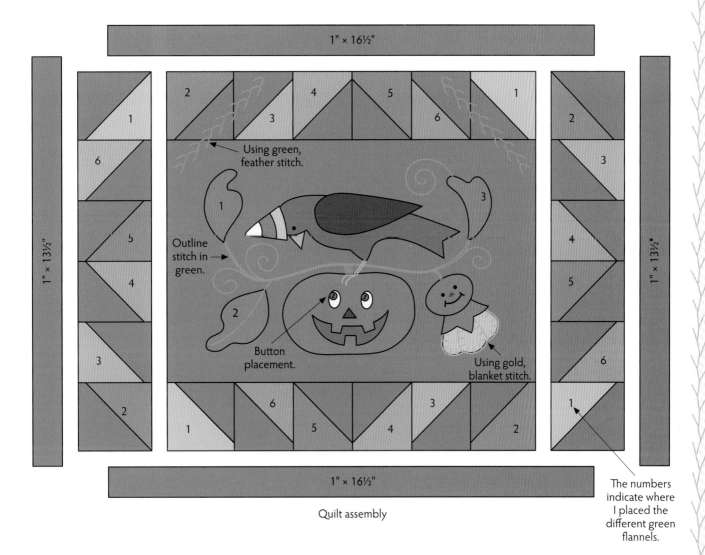

Quilt assembly

1" × 16½"

1" × 13½"

1" × 13½"

1" × 16½"

Using green, feather stitch.

Outline stitch in green.

Button placement.

Using gold, blanket stitch.

The numbers indicate where I placed the different green flannels.

3  Referring to the assembly diagram above, make four patchwork borders using six half-square-triangle units each. The numbers in the diagram refer to the six different green flannels to help you mix them up for a scrappy border.

4  Sew the top and bottom borders to the appliquéd center. Then sew the remaining borders to the sides of the appliquéd center. Press. Stay stitch around the perimeter, about ⅛" from the edges.

5  Using Olive Green pearl cotton, feather stitch through the centers of the black flannel diagonal lines formed by the half-square-triangle units.

## finishing

To complete the project as shown, refer to "Finishing Techniques" on page 58. You will need the black flannel 1" × 13½" and 1" × 16½" strips as well as the two black flannel 9¼" × 13½" rectangles.

Alternately, if you prefer to join the 12 appliqué pieces into one large quilt, turn to "All Year with Bertie" on page 59 for sashing and border cutting instructions and assembly directions for two quilt options.

# November

*Bertie is getting ready for the cold months.*
*When the leaves begin to turn shades of orange and red,*
*it's time to pick the last tasty berries from the garden.*

■ FINISHED SIZE: 13" × 17"

## materials

*This project was made using Woolies flannels from Maywood Studio with wool appliqué.*

½ yard of espresso houndstooth (black) flannel for background, borders, and backing

2 squares, 3" × 3" *each*, of 6 assorted orange and gold flannels for patchwork border (12 squares total)

3" × 7" piece of light brown wool for bird

2" × 4" piece of medium brown herringbone, tweed, or plaid wool for bird's wing

4" × 4" square *each*, of 2 different rust plaid wools for leaves 1 and 3

2" × 4" piece of goldish green wool for leaf 2

4" × 4" square of light olive green wool for leaf 4

2" × 10" piece of brown wool for branches

3" × 4" piece of blue plaid wool for scarf

1" × 1" square of gold wool for beak

3 red buttons (½" or ⅝" diameter) for berries

13½" × 17½" piece of lightweight batting

Sewing thread or embroidery floss in colors to match wool-appliqué pieces

Size 12 Valdani pearl cotton for embroidery details:
■ P2 Olive Green
■ P5 Tarnished Gold
■ 1 Black Dyed

Fusible web

## cutting

**From the black flannel, refer to the cutting guide below to cut:**
■ 2 pieces, 9¼" × 13½"
■ 1 piece, 9" × 13"
■ 2 strips, 1" × 16½"
■ 2 strips, 1" × 13½"
■ 12 squares, 3" × 3"

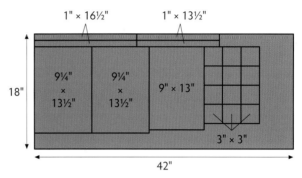

Cutting guide for black flannel

## preparing appliqué pieces

Trace the appliqué patterns (page 77) onto fusible web. The pieces are already reversed so you can trace directly on the paper backing of the fusible web. Loosely cut around the traced shapes. Iron the fusible shapes onto the *wrong* side of the wool (choose the side you like best for the right side) in the colors indicated on the pattern pieces. Then cut out the pieces on the traced lines.

## appliquéing the design

1 Arrange the appliqués on the black flannel 9" × 13" piece. The background will be trimmed to 8½" × 12½" after the appliqué is complete, so be sure to keep the shapes within these dimensions. Tuck some pieces under others as indicated on the assembly diagram on page 53. When satisfied with the placement, fuse all the pieces in place.

2 Whipstitch the pieces to the background using matching thread. Try to keep the stitches about ⅛" apart and ⅛" deep into the appliqués. Keep the stitches perpendicular to the edges of the shapes.

3 Referring to "Embroidery Stitches" on page 8 as needed, use pearl cotton to add embroidery details:

- Using Tarnished Gold, make a double row of outline stitches for the bird's leg and a single row of outline stitches for the foot. Also outline stitch a single row for the veins and stems of the leaves.

- Using Olive Green, outline stitch the stems of the berries in the bird's beak.

- Using Black Dyed, stitch a French knot for the bird's eye.

## adding the border

1 Press the design and trim the appliquéd center to 8½" × 12½", trimming evenly all around the piece.

2 Draw a diagonal line from corner to corner on the wrong side of the orange and gold flannel 3" squares. Pair each orange and gold square with a black flannel square, right sides together. Stitch ¼" from each side of the drawn lines and then cut apart on the drawn lines to make 24 half-square-triangle units. Press the seam allowances open and trim the units to 2½" square.

| Sew ¼" from both sides of the drawn line. | Cut apart on the drawn line. | Press seam allowances open and trim blocks to 2½". |

3 Referring to the assembly diagram on page 53, make four patchwork borders using six half-square-triangle units each. Notice that the two side borders have the end triangles facing in a different direction than those on the top and bottom borders. The numbers in the diagram refer to the six different orange and gold flannels to help you mix them up for a scrappy border.

4 Sew the top and bottom borders to the appliquéd center. Then sew the remaining borders to the sides of the appliquéd center. Press. Stay stitch around the perimeter, about ⅛" from the edges.

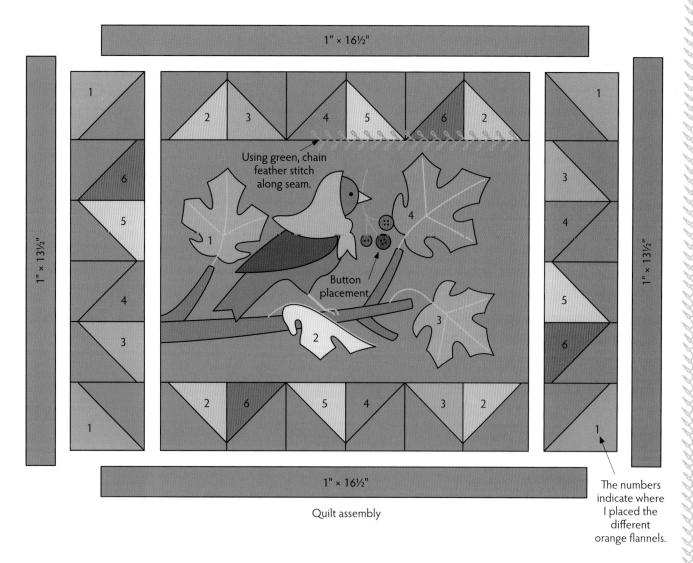

1" × 16½"

1" × 13½"

1" × 13½"

Using green, chain feather stitch along seam.

Button placement.

1" × 16½"

Quilt assembly

The numbers indicate where I placed the different orange flannels.

5 Using Olive Green pearl cotton, make a chained feather stitch along the seamline where the pieced border meets the appliqué background.

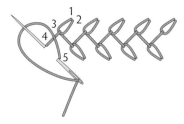

Chained feather stitch

6 Using black thread, sew the three buttons to the quilt top for berries.

# finishing

To complete the project as shown, refer to "Finishing Techniques" on page 58. You will need the black flannel 1" × 13½" and 1" × 16½" strips as well as the two black flannel 9¼" × 13½" rectangles.

Alternately, if you prefer to join the 12 appliqué pieces into one large quilt, turn to "All Year with Bertie" on page 59 for sashing and border cutting instructions and assembly directions for two quilt options.

# December

*Deck the boughs for the holidays! The sky is filled with snowflakes, so it's a good thing Bertie's wearing a festive red muffler while enjoying the holiday decor.*

■ FINISHED SIZE: 13" × 17"

# materials

*This project was made using Woolies flannels from Maywood Studio with wool appliqué.*

½ yard of espresso houndstooth (black) flannel for background, borders, and backing

2 squares, 3" × 3" *each*, of 5 assorted red flannels for patchwork border (10 squares total)

3" × 7" piece of light brown wool for bird

2" × 4" piece of medium brown herringbone, tweed, or plaid wool for bird's wing

2" × 10" piece of brown wool for branches

6" × 7" piece of green wool for pine needle bunches

3" × 3" square of red wool for ornament

2" × 3" piece of off-white wool for ornament band

1" × 1" square of gray wool for ornament cap

1" × 1" square of gold wool for beak

2" × 4" piece of red plaid wool for scarf

13½" × 17½" piece of lightweight batting

Sewing thread or embroidery floss in colors to match wool-appliqué pieces

Size 12 Valdani pearl cotton for embroidery details:
- O178 Tea-Dyed Stone
- P1 Old Brick
- P4 Aged White
- P5 Tarnished Gold
- 1 Black Dyed

Fusible web

FriXion heat-erasable marking pen (optional)

# cutting

**From the black flannel, refer to the cutting guide below to cut:**
- 2 pieces, 9¼" × 13½"
- 1 piece, 9" × 13"
- 2 strips, 1" × 16½"
- 2 strips, 1" × 13½"
- 10 squares, 3" × 3"
- 4 squares, 2½" × 2½"

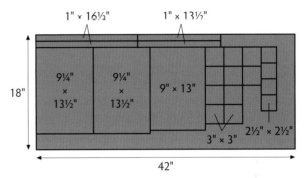

Cutting guide for black flannel

# preparing appliqué pieces

Trace the appliqué patterns (pages 78 and 79) onto fusible web. The pieces are already reversed so you can trace directly on the paper backing of the fusible web. Loosely cut around the traced shapes. Iron the fusible shapes onto the *wrong* side of the wool (choose the side you like best for the right side) in the colors indicated on the pattern pieces. Then cut out the pieces on the traced lines.

# appliquéing the design

1 Arrange the appliqués on the black flannel 9" × 13" piece. The background will be trimmed to 8½" × 12½" after the appliqué is complete, so be sure to keep the shapes within these dimensions. Tuck some pieces under others as indicated on the assembly diagram on page 57. When satisfied with the placement, fuse all the pieces in place.

2 Whipstitch the pieces to the background using matching thread. Try to keep the stitches about ⅛" apart and ⅛" deep into the appliqués. Keep the stitches perpendicular to the edges of the shapes.

3 Referring to "Embroidery Stitches" on page 8 as needed, use pearl cotton to add embroidery details:

- Using Tarnished Gold, make a double row of outline stitches for the bird's leg and a single row of outline stitches for the foot.

- Using Black Dyed, stitch a French knot for the bird's eye.

- Using Tea-Dyed Stone, make a lazy daisy stitch for the ornament hanging loop. Outline stitch the ornament hook.

- Using Old Brick, outline stitch the lettering on the ornament. Note: If you prefer, you can use a FriXion pen to write Noel on the off-white wool before embroidering. Any visible pen marks left after stitching the letters will disappear when you iron them.

- Using Aged White and straight stitches, add snowflakes in the background.

## adding the border

1 Press the design and trim the appliquéd center to 8½" × 12½", trimming evenly all around the piece.

2 Draw a diagonal line from corner to corner on the wrong side of the red flannel 3" squares. Pair each red square with a black flannel square, right sides together. Stitch ¼" from each side of the drawn lines and then cut apart on the drawn lines to make 20 half-square-triangle units. Press the seam allowances open and trim the units to 2½" square.

Sew ¼" from both sides of the drawn line.

Cut apart on the drawn line.

Press seam allowances open and trim blocks to 2½".

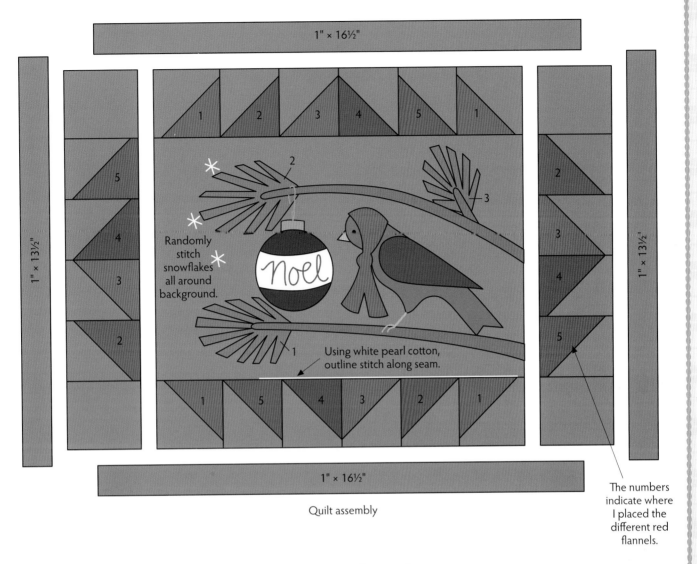

1" × 16½"

1" × 13½"

1" × 13½"

Randomly stitch snowflakes all around background.

*noel*

Using white pearl cotton, outline stitch along seam.

1" × 16½"

Quilt assembly

The numbers indicate where I placed the different red flannels.

**3** Referring to the assembly diagram above, make two patchwork borders using six half-square-triangle units each and two borders using four half-square-triangle units each. The numbers in the diagram refer to the five different red flannels to help you mix them up for a scrappy border.

**4** Sew the top and bottom borders to the appliquéd center. Sew a black 2½" square the ends of the side borders and then sew them to the appliquéd center. Press. Stay stitch around the perimeter, about ⅛" from the edges.

**5** Using Aged White pearl cotton, outline stitch along the seamline where the pieced border meets the appliqué background.

# finishing

To complete the project as shown, refer to "Finishing Techniques" on page 58. You will need the black flannel 1" × 13½" and 1" × 16½" strips as well as the two black flannel 9¼" × 13½" rectangles.

Alternately, if you prefer to join the 12 appliqué pieces into one large quilt, turn to "All Year with Bertie" on page 59 for sashing and border cutting instructions and assembly directions for two quilt options.

# Finishing Techniques

All of the 13" × 17" monthly Bertie wall hangings are finished in the same manner. If you prefer to use traditional binding, you will need additional yardage. But I encourage you to try my easy pillowcase finish. After the project is turned right side out, I stitch in the ditch of the border to create the look of binding, without the fuss.

1   For the backing, use a ½" seam allowance to sew the two 9¼" × 13½" rectangles together. Sew along one 13½"-long edge and leave 3" to 4" unsewn in the center of the seam for turning. Press the seam allowances open.

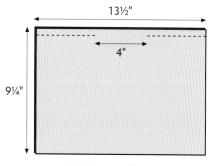

Use ½" seam allowance.
Leave 3" to 4" unsewn.

2   Cut a 13½" × 17½" piece of batting. Lay the batting on your work table. Place the quilt top on the batting, *right side up.* Then place the prepared back on top, *right side down.* (The appliqué and the backing are right sides together.)

3   Using a ¼" seam allowance and your machine's walking foot or even-feed system, sew through all layers all the way around the piece. Clip the excess fabric and batting from the corners, then turn

the piece right side out through the opening in the backing seam. Press the piece flat and then hand sew the opening closed.

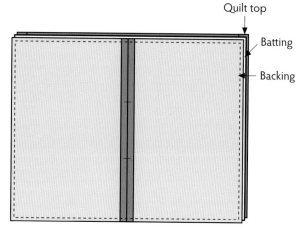

Stitch ¼" from edge all the way around quilt.

4   From the right side of the quilt, stitch in the ditch where the outer black flannel border and the pieced border meet. The result looks like binding, without having to make and attach binding!

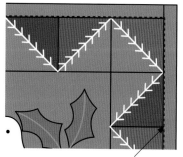

Stitch in the ditch where the outer border meets the pieced border, making the look of binding.

# All Year with Bertie: Throw

*If you'd prefer to gather all the Bertie's Year appliqués into one large quilt, here are instructions for cutting flannel sashing and binding and joining the appliqués into a beautiful throw.*

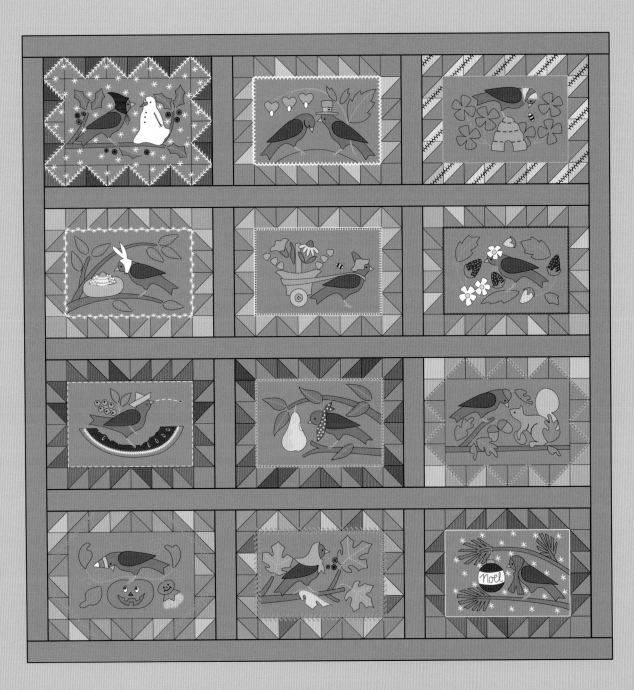

 FINISHED SIZE: 56½" × 58½"

## additional materials

*In addition to the materials for each monthly appliqué block, you'll need the following:*

1¾ yards of black flannel for sashing and binding

3½ yards of flannel or cotton for backing

63" × 65" piece of batting

## cutting

**From the black flannel, cut:**
- 19 strips, 2½" × 42"; crosscut *3 of the strips* into 8 strips, 2½" × 12½"

**Join 10 of the remaining strips end to end and cut into:**
- 2 strips, 2½" × 56½"
- 2 strips, 2½" × 54½"
- 3 strips, 2½" × 52½"

**Reserve the remaining 2½" strips for binding.**

## assembling the quilt top

Press all seam allowances toward the flannel sashing strips.

1 Appliqué each of the monthly blocks per their instructions. *Do not attach the 1"-wide black border strips.*

2 Lay out the appliquéd blocks in four rows of three blocks each, placing a black flannel 2½" × 12½" strip between the blocks in each row. Sew the rows together; press. Make three rows, 12½" × 52½".

3 Join the block rows with the 2½" × 52½" sashing strips; press. The quilt center should measure 52½" × 54½".

4 Sew the black flannel 54½" strips to the left and right edges of the quilt top. Press. Add the 56½"-long flannel strips to the top and bottom of the quilt. Press. The completed quilt top should measure 56½" × 58½".

5 Quilt as desired. Trim the batting and backing even with the quilt top edges and bind using the remaining 2½"-wide flannel strips.

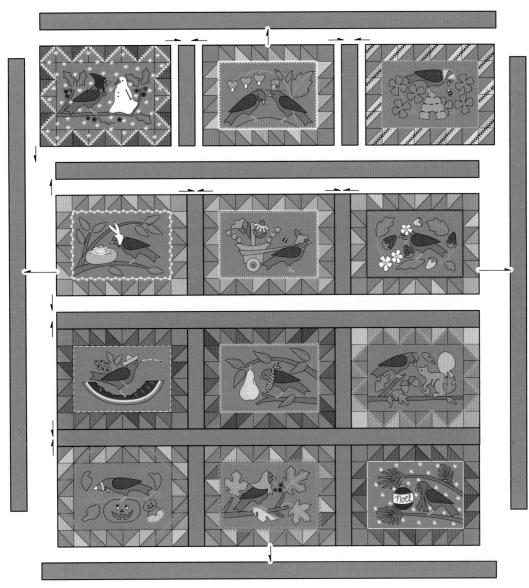

Quilt assembly

# All Year with Bertie: Wall Hanging

*For this slightly smaller wall hanging, you'll need all 12 months of the Bertie's Year appliqué blocks, but don't attach the pieced borders from the individual patterns. Instead, you'll be making half-square-triangle sashing. The sample uses assorted green flannels, but choose whatever color you prefer.*

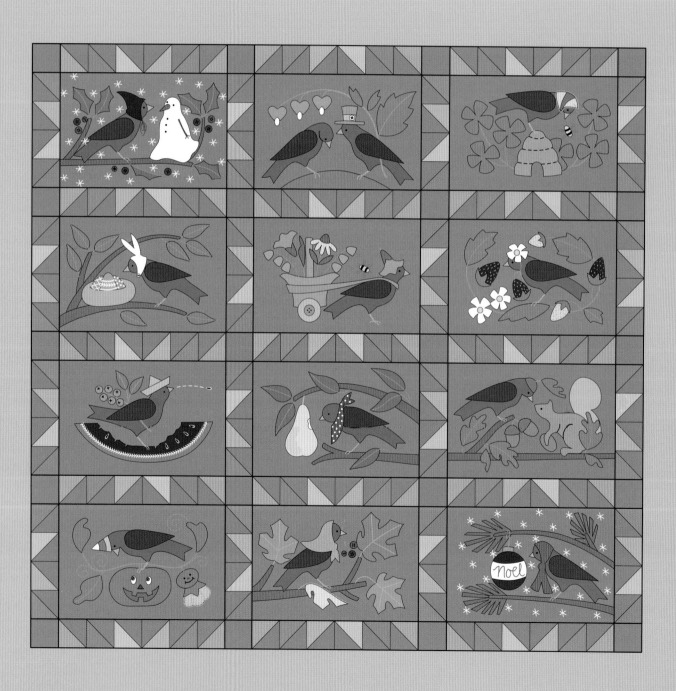

■ FINISHED SIZE: 44½" × 42½"

## additional materials

*You'll appliqué each of the 12 blocks, but you do not need all of the extra flannels for the pieced borders. Instead, here's what you'll use:*

6 fat quarters of assorted green flannels for sashing

½ yard of black flannel for binding

2¾ yards of flannel or cotton for backing

49" × 51" piece of batting

## cutting

**From the assorted green flannels, cut a *total* of:**
- 79 squares, 3" × 3"

**From the black flannel (left over from each month's pattern), cut a *total* of:**
- 79 squares, 3" × 3"
- 20 squares, 2½" × 2½"

**From the black flannel for binding, cut:**
- 6 strips, 2½" × 42"

## making the sashing

1 Draw a diagonal line from corner to corner on the back of each green 3" square. Pair each green square with a black 3" square and sew ¼" from each side of the drawn lines. Cut apart on the drawn lines to make 158 half-square-triangle units (4 are extra). Press the seam allowances open and trim the units to 2½" square.

| Sew ¼" from both sides of the drawn line. | Cut apart on the drawn line. | Press seam allowances open and trim blocks to 2½". |

2 Choose six half-square-triangle units, each with a different green flannel. Sew the units together as shown to make a strip that measures 2½" × 12½". Make 15 strips. In the same manner, join four half-square-triangle units to make a short sashing strip that measures 2½" × 8½". Make 16 strips.

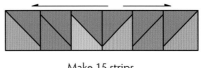

Make 15 strips, 2½" × 12½".

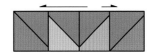

Make 16 strips, 2½" × 8½".

## assembling the quilt top

1 Lay out the appliqué blocks in four rows of three blocks each, leaving 2½" between blocks for sashing.

2 Lay out the longer sashing strips above and below the appliqué blocks, noting that the direction of the triangles alternates from block to block; on one block the green triangles are against the appliqué, and on the next block, the black triangles are against the appliqué. Place the black 2½" squares between the sashing strips in each row as well as at the beginning and end of the row. Sew the sashing strips and black squares together to make five sashing rows.

3 Lay out the short sashing strips along the sides of the appliqué blocks, again noting the orientation of the triangles. Sew the short sashing strips and appliqué blocks together in rows, pressing the seam allowances toward the appliqué.

4  Sew the rows together to complete the quilt top, which should measure 44½" × 42½". Press.

5  Quilt as desired. Trim the batting and backing even with the quilt top edges and bind using the 2½"-wide flannel strips.

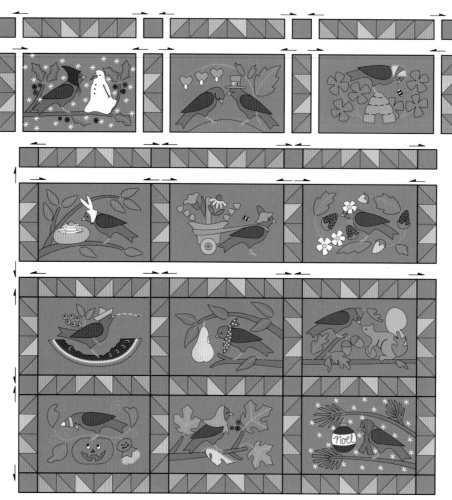

Quilt assembly

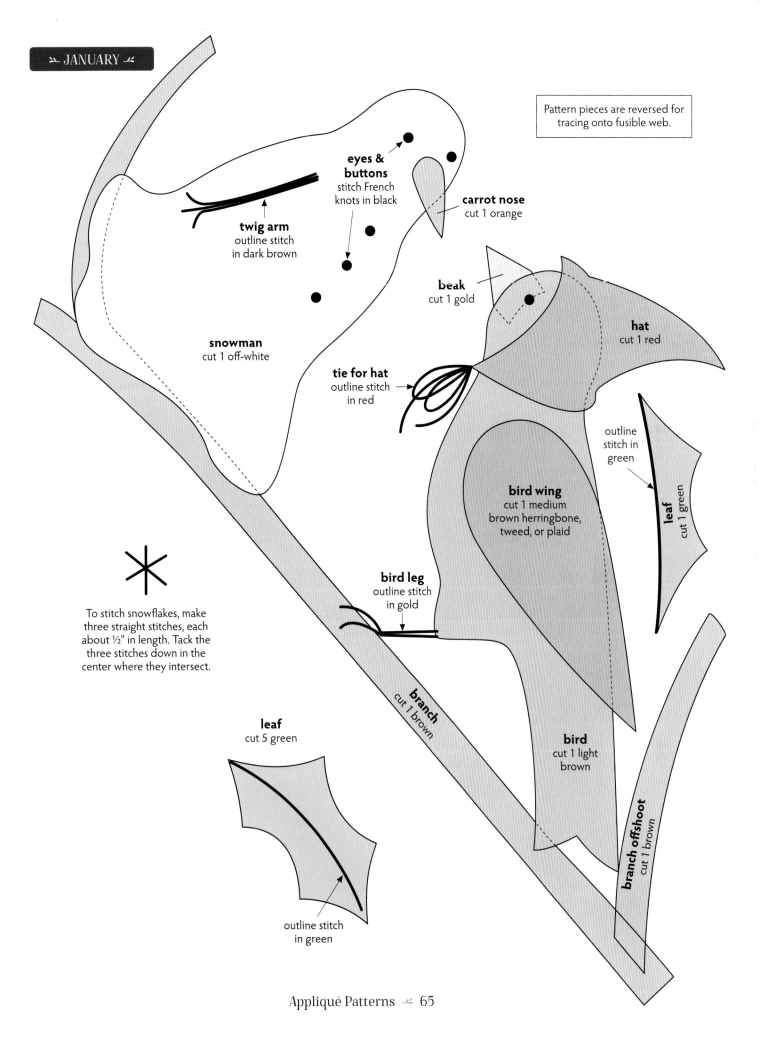

Pattern pieces are reversed for tracing onto fusible web.

**eyes & buttons**
stitch French knots in black

**carrot nose**
cut 1 orange

**twig arm**
outline stitch in dark brown

**beak**
cut 1 gold

**hat**
cut 1 red

**snowman**
cut 1 off-white

**tie for hat**
outline stitch in red

outline stitch in green

**leaf**
cut 1 green

**bird wing**
cut 1 medium brown herringbone, tweed, or plaid

**bird leg**
outline stitch in gold

To stitch snowflakes, make three straight stitches, each about ½" in length. Tack the three stitches down in the center where they intersect.

**branch**
cut 1 brown

**bird**
cut 1 light brown

**branch offshoot**
cut 1 brown

**leaf**
cut 5 green

outline stitch in green

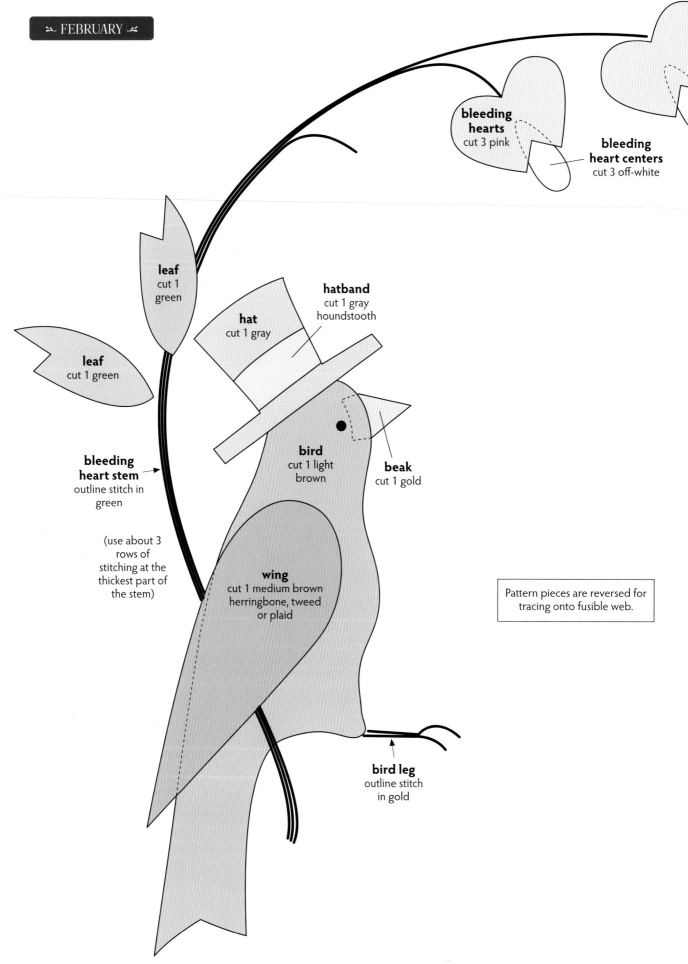

**bleeding hearts**
cut 3 pink

**bleeding heart centers**
cut 3 off-white

**leaf**
cut 1 green

**leaf**
cut 1 green

**hatband**
cut 1 gray
houndstooth

**hat**
cut 1 gray

**bleeding heart stem**
outline stitch in green

(use about 3 rows of stitching at the thickest part of the stem)

**bird**
cut 1 light brown

**beak**
cut 1 gold

**wing**
cut 1 medium brown herringbone, tweed or plaid

Pattern pieces are reversed for tracing onto fusible web.

**bird leg**
outline stitch in gold

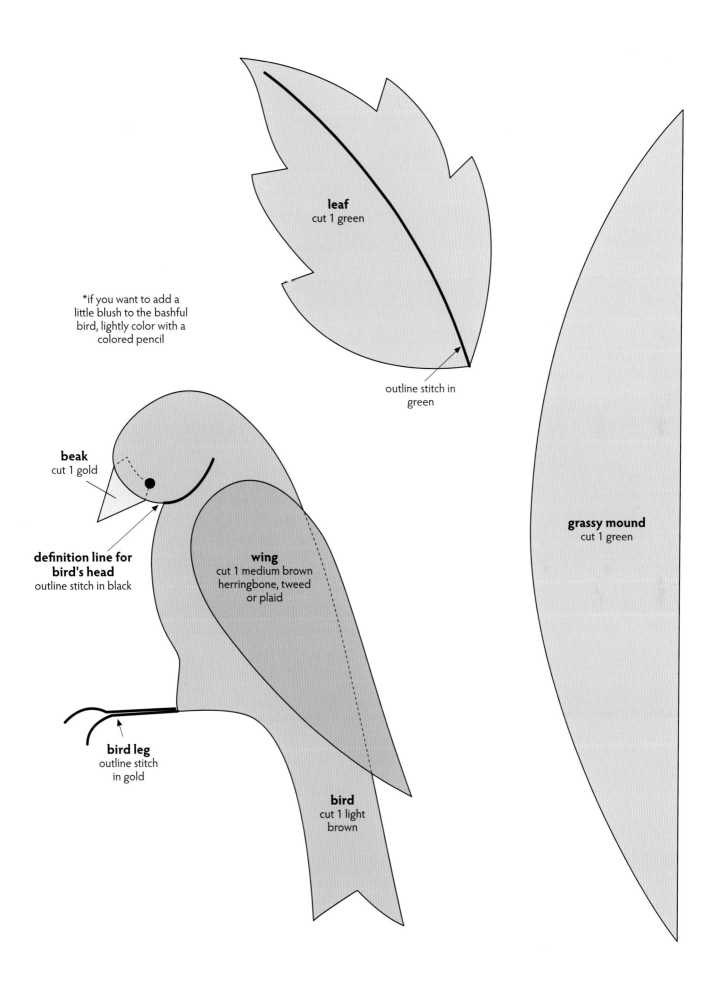

leaf
cut 1 green

outline stitch in
green

*if you want to add a
little blush to the bashful
bird, lightly color with a
colored pencil

beak
cut 1 gold

definition line for
bird's head
outline stitch in black

bird leg
outline stitch
in gold

wing
cut 1 medium brown
herringbone, tweed
or plaid

bird
cut 1 light
brown

grassy mound
cut 1 green

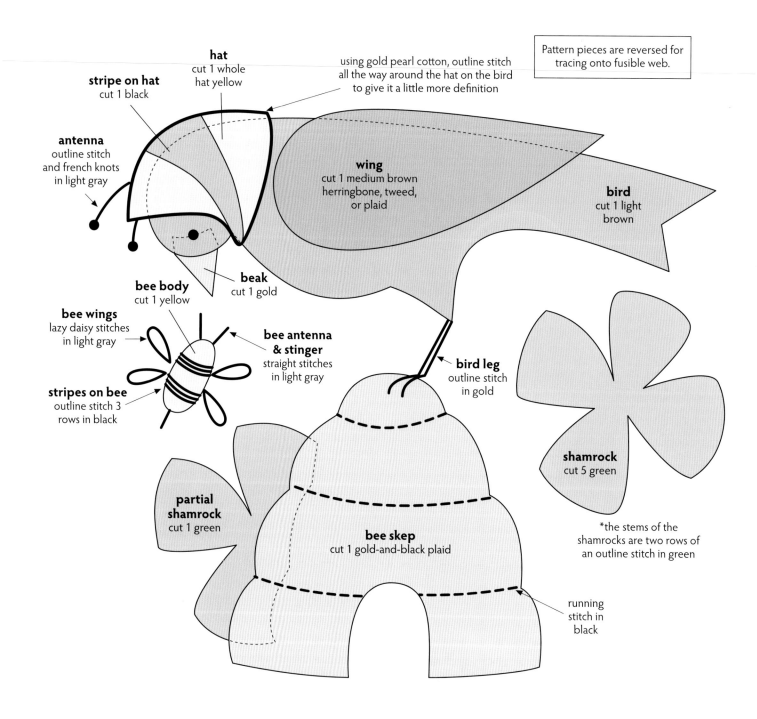

**hat**
cut 1 whole
hat yellow

**stripe on hat**
cut 1 black

using gold pearl cotton, outline stitch
all the way around the hat on the bird
to give it a little more definition

Pattern pieces are reversed for
tracing onto fusible web.

**antenna**
outline stitch
and french knots
in light gray

**wing**
cut 1 medium brown
herringbone, tweed,
or plaid

**bird**
cut 1 light
brown

**bee body**
cut 1 yellow

**beak**
cut 1 gold

**bee wings**
lazy daisy stitches
in light gray

**bee antenna
& stinger**
straight stitches
in light gray

**stripes on bee**
outline stitch 3
rows in black

**bird leg**
outline stitch
in gold

**shamrock**
cut 5 green

**partial
shamrock**
cut 1 green

**bee skep**
cut 1 gold-and-black plaid

*the stems of the
shamrocks are two rows of
an outline stitch in green

running
stitch in
black

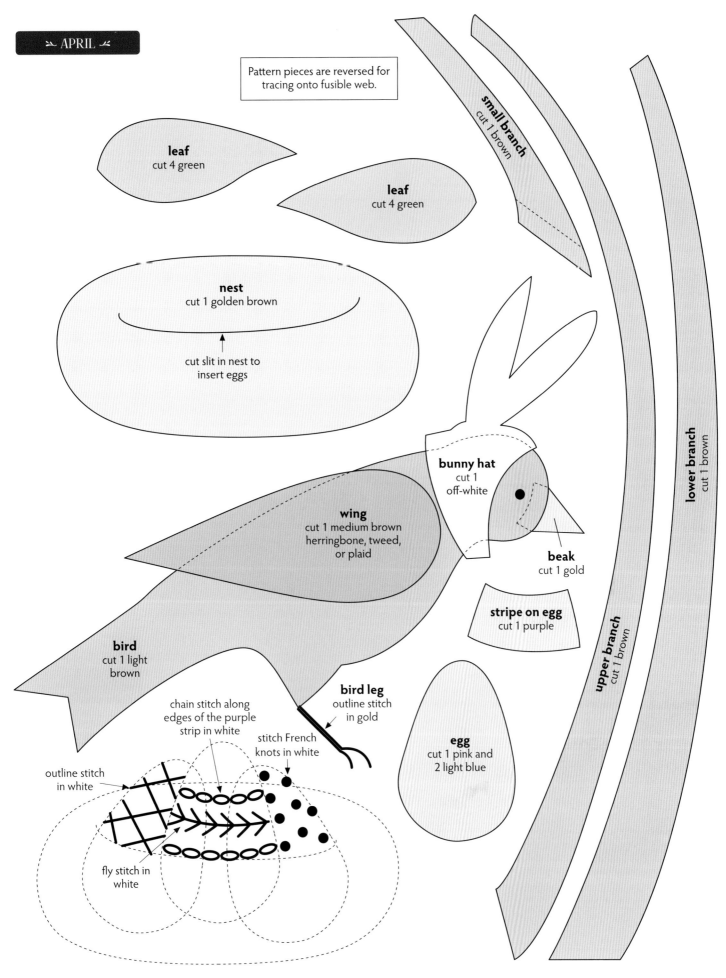

Pattern pieces are reversed for tracing onto fusible web.

**leaf**
cut 4 green

**leaf**
cut 4 green

**small branch**
cut 1 brown

**nest**
cut 1 golden brown

cut slit in nest to
insert eggs

**bunny hat**
cut 1
off-white

**wing**
cut 1 medium brown
herringbone, tweed,
or plaid

**beak**
cut 1 gold

**stripe on egg**
cut 1 purple

**lower branch**
cut 1 brown

**bird**
cut 1 light
brown

**upper branch**
cut 1 brown

**bird leg**
outline stitch
in gold

chain stitch along
edges of the purple
strip in white

stitch French
knots in white

outline stitch
in white

**egg**
cut 1 pink and
2 light blue

fly stitch in
white

Appliqué Patterns ~ 69

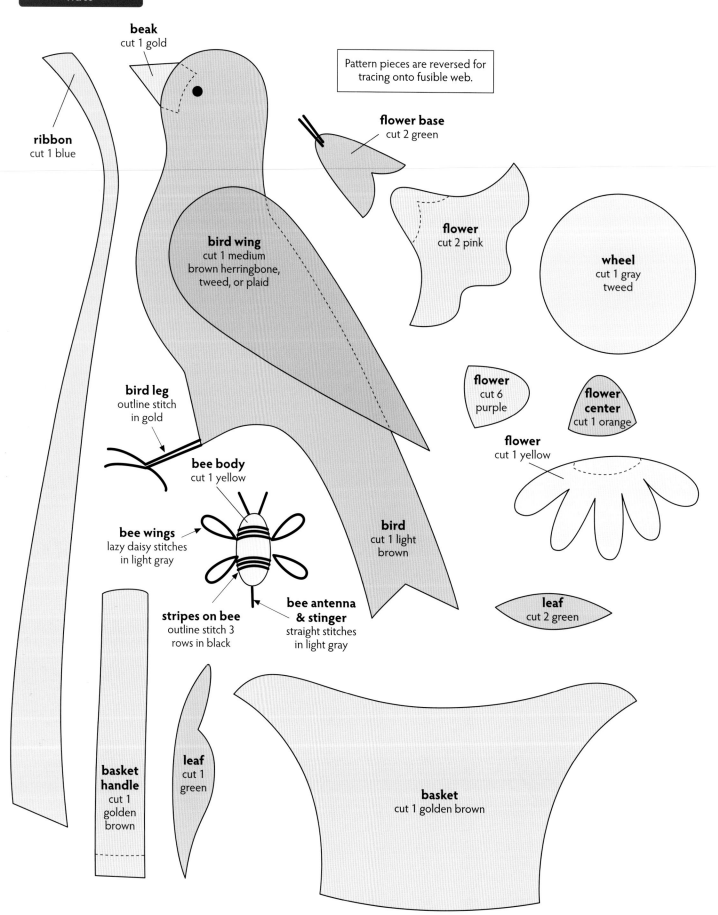

**beak**
cut 1 gold

Pattern pieces are reversed for tracing onto fusible web.

**flower base**
cut 2 green

**ribbon**
cut 1 blue

**bird wing**
cut 1 medium brown herringbone, tweed, or plaid

**flower**
cut 2 pink

**wheel**
cut 1 gray tweed

**flower**
cut 6 purple

**flower center**
cut 1 orange

**flower**
cut 1 yellow

**bird leg**
outline stitch in gold

**bee body**
cut 1 yellow

**bee wings**
lazy daisy stitches in light gray

**bird**
cut 1 light brown

**stripes on bee**
outline stitch 3 rows in black

**bee antenna & stinger**
straight stitches in light gray

**leaf**
cut 2 green

**basket handle**
cut 1 golden brown

**leaf**
cut 1 green

**basket**
cut 1 golden brown

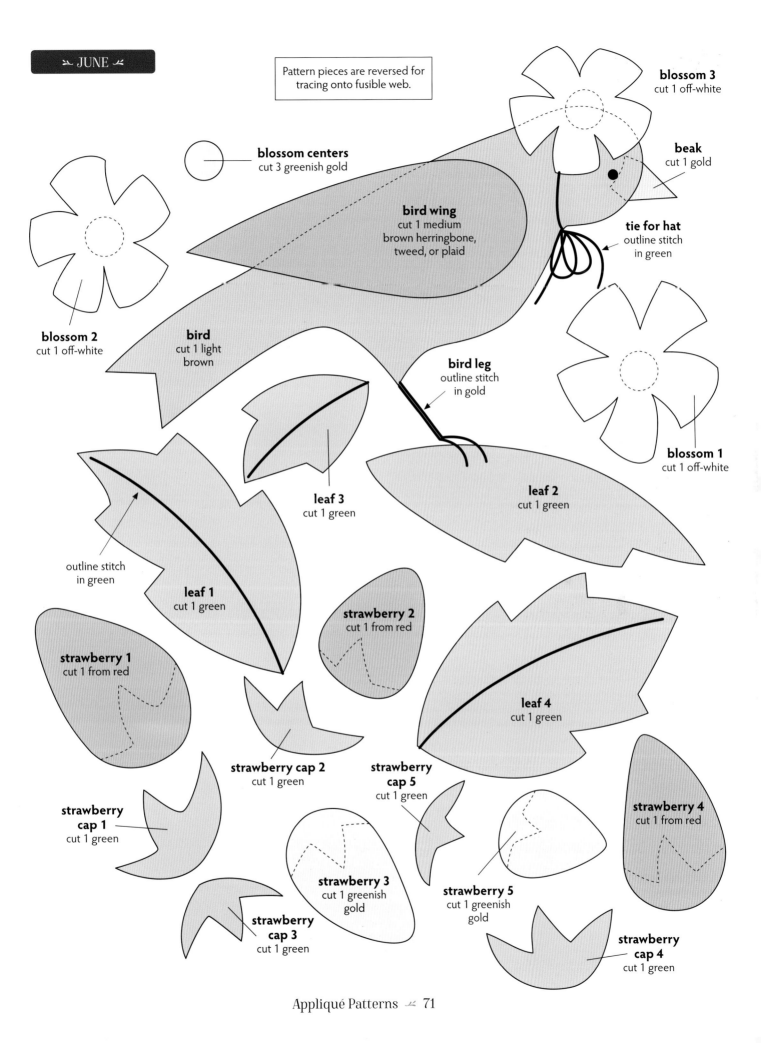

Pattern pieces are reversed for tracing onto fusible web.

blossom 3
cut 1 off-white

blossom centers
cut 3 greenish gold

beak
cut 1 gold

bird wing
cut 1 medium
brown herringbone,
tweed, or plaid

tie for hat
outline stitch
in green

blossom 2
cut 1 off-white

bird
cut 1 light
brown

bird leg
outline stitch
in gold

blossom 1
cut 1 off-white

leaf 3
cut 1 green

leaf 2
cut 1 green

outline stitch
in green

leaf 1
cut 1 green

strawberry 2
cut 1 from red

leaf 4
cut 1 green

strawberry 1
cut 1 from red

strawberry cap 2
cut 1 green

strawberry
cap 5
cut 1 green

strawberry 4
cut 1 from red

strawberry
cap 1
cut 1 green

strawberry 3
cut 1 greenish
gold

strawberry 5
cut 1 greenish
gold

strawberry
cap 3
cut 1 green

strawberry
cap 4
cut 1 green

Appliqué Patterns ⤙ 71

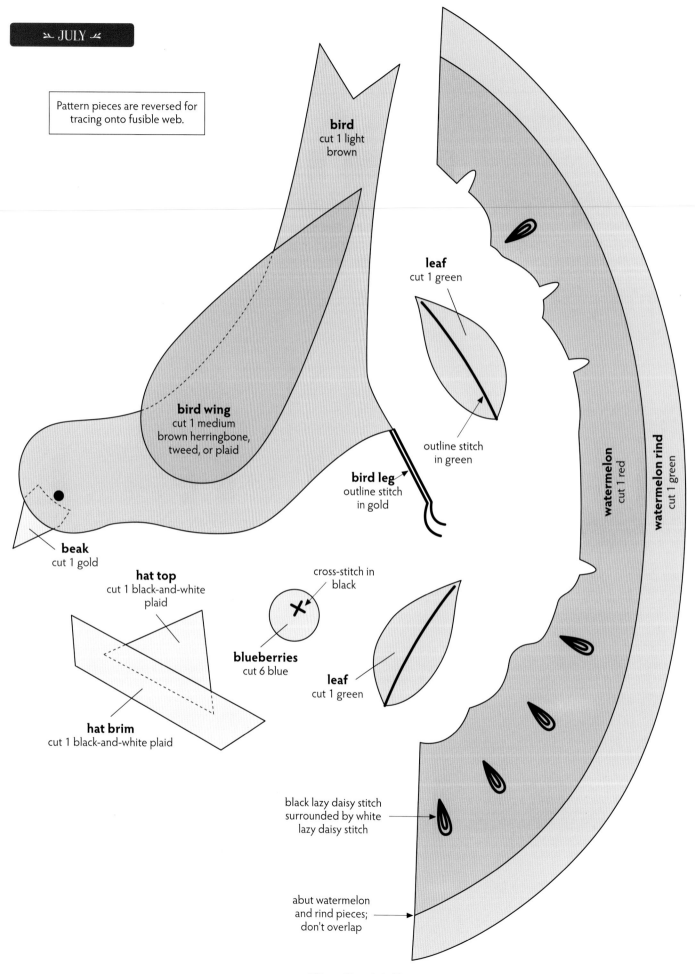

Pattern pieces are reversed for tracing onto fusible web.

**bird**
cut 1 light brown

**leaf**
cut 1 green

outline stitch in green

**bird wing**
cut 1 medium brown herringbone, tweed, or plaid

**bird leg**
outline stitch in gold

**beak**
cut 1 gold

**watermelon**
cut 1 red

**watermelon rind**
cut 1 green

**hat top**
cut 1 black-and-white plaid

cross-stitch in black

**blueberries**
cut 6 blue

**leaf**
cut 1 green

**hat brim**
cut 1 black-and-white plaid

black lazy daisy stitch surrounded by white lazy daisy stitch

abut watermelon and rind pieces; don't overlap

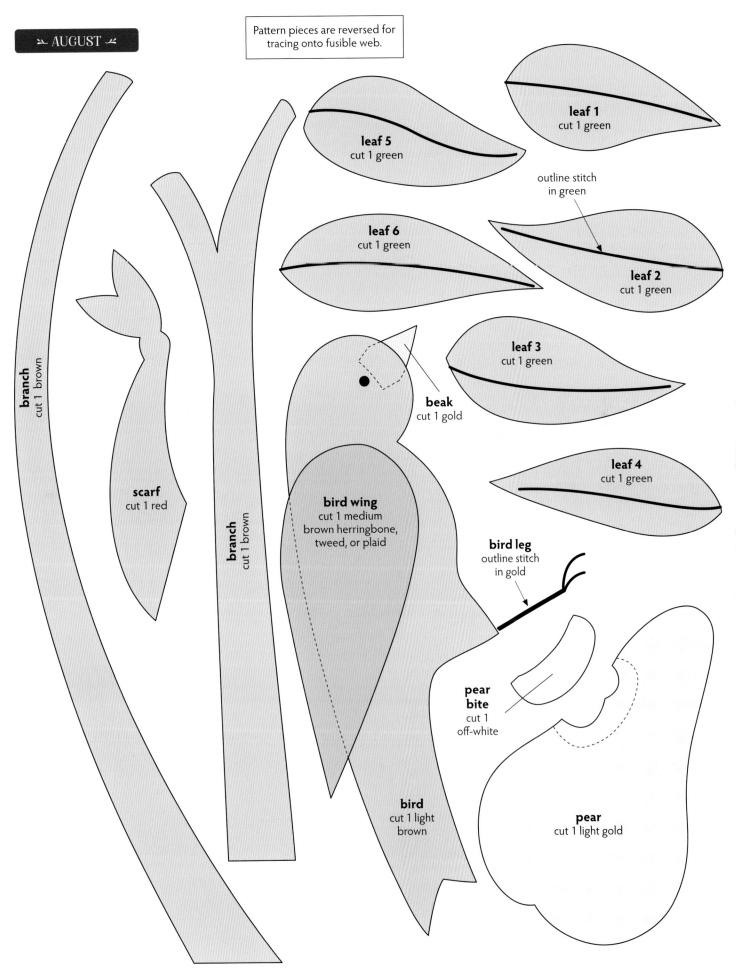

Pattern pieces are reversed for tracing onto fusible web.

**leaf 1**
cut 1 green

**leaf 5**
cut 1 green

outline stitch in green

**leaf 6**
cut 1 green

**leaf 2**
cut 1 green

**leaf 3**
cut 1 green

**beak**
cut 1 gold

**branch**
cut 1 brown

**leaf 4**
cut 1 green

**scarf**
cut 1 red

**bird wing**
cut 1 medium brown herringbone, tweed, or plaid

**bird leg**
outline stitch in gold

**branch**
cut 1 brown

**pear bite**
cut 1 off-white

**bird**
cut 1 light brown

**pear**
cut 1 light gold

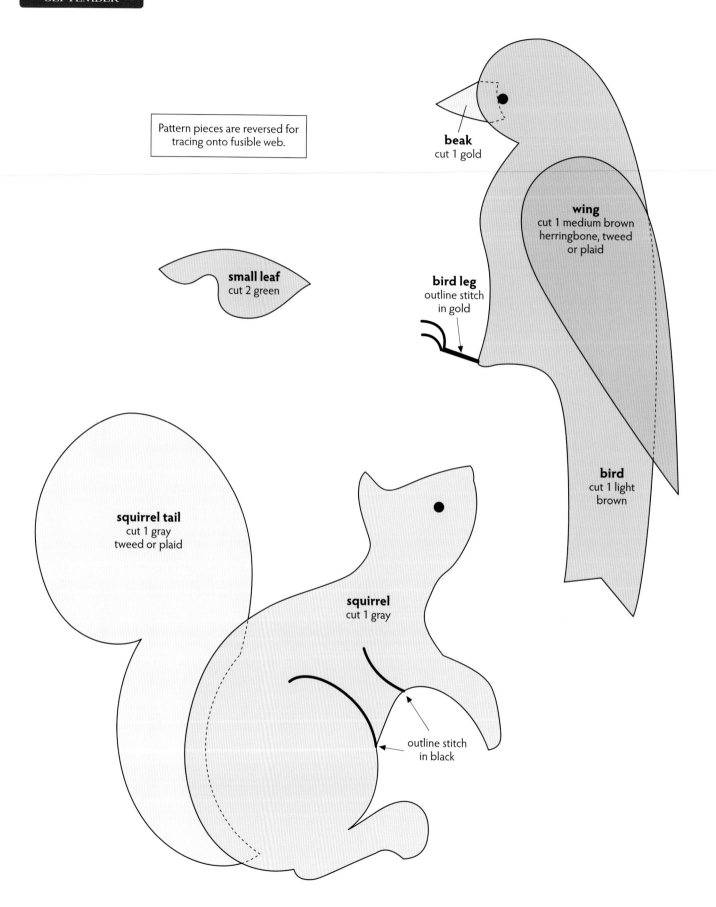

Pattern pieces are reversed for tracing onto fusible web.

**beak**
cut 1 gold

**wing**
cut 1 medium brown
herringbone, tweed
or plaid

**small leaf**
cut 2 green

**bird leg**
outline stitch
in gold

**bird**
cut 1 light
brown

**squirrel tail**
cut 1 gray
tweed or plaid

**squirrel**
cut 1 gray

outline stitch
in black

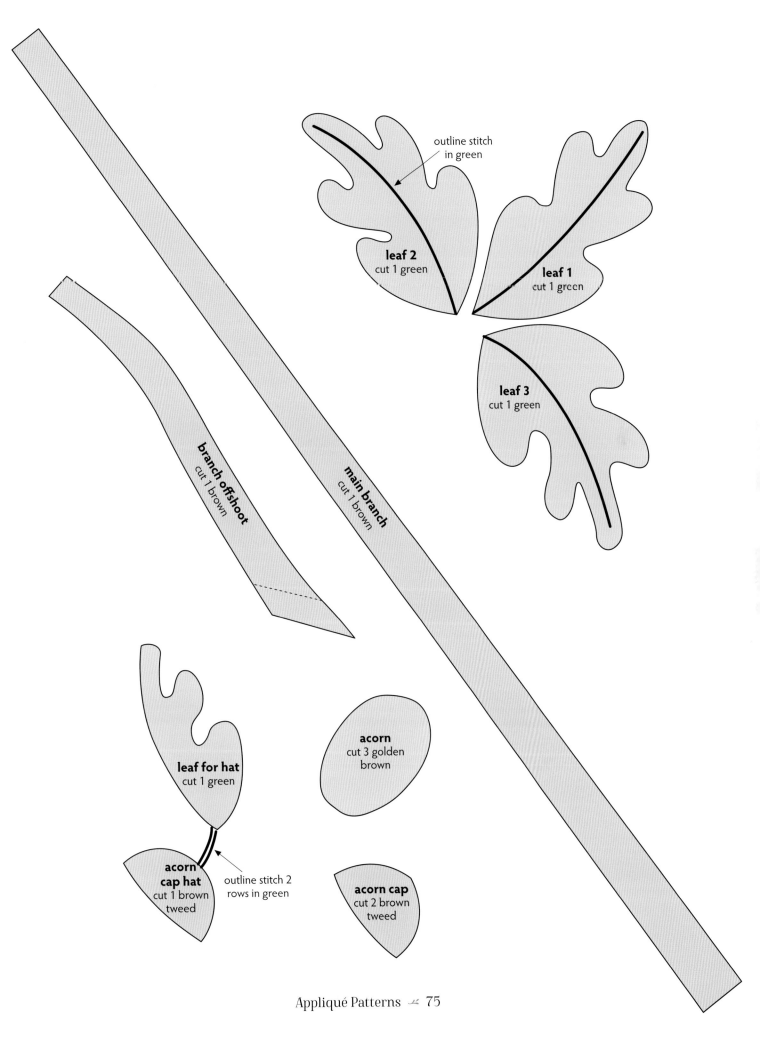

outline stitch
in green

**leaf 2**
cut 1 green

**leaf 1**
cut 1 green

**leaf 3**
cut 1 green

**branch offshoot**
cut 1 brown

**main branch**
cut 1 brown

**leaf for hat**
cut 1 green

**acorn**
cut 3 golden
brown

**acorn
cap hat**
cut 1 brown
tweed

outline stitch 2
rows in green

**acorn cap**
cut 2 brown
tweed

Appliqué Patterns ⤳ 75

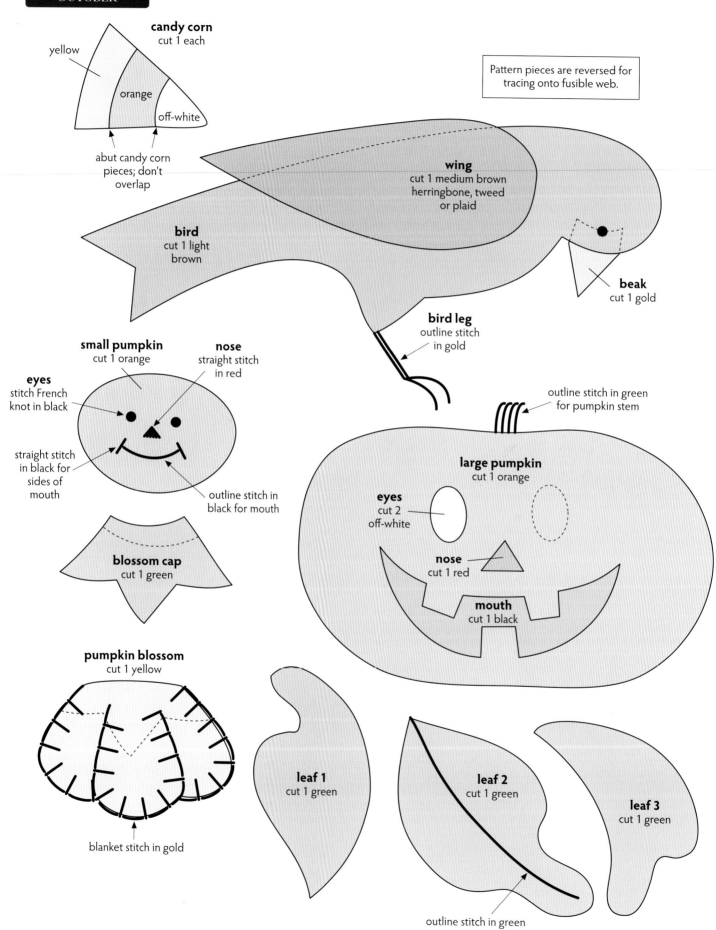

**candy corn**
cut 1 each

yellow

orange

off-white

abut candy corn
pieces; don't
overlap

Pattern pieces are reversed for
tracing onto fusible web.

**wing**
cut 1 medium brown
herringbone, tweed
or plaid

**bird**
cut 1 light
brown

**beak**
cut 1 gold

**bird leg**
outline stitch
in gold

**small pumpkin**
cut 1 orange

**nose**
straight stitch
in red

**eyes**
stitch French
knot in black

straight stitch
in black for
sides of
mouth

outline stitch in
black for mouth

outline stitch in green
for pumpkin stem

**large pumpkin**
cut 1 orange

**eyes**
cut 2
off-white

**nose**
cut 1 red

**mouth**
cut 1 black

**blossom cap**
cut 1 green

**pumpkin blossom**
cut 1 yellow

blanket stitch in gold

**leaf 1**
cut 1 green

**leaf 2**
cut 1 green

**leaf 3**
cut 1 green

outline stitch in green

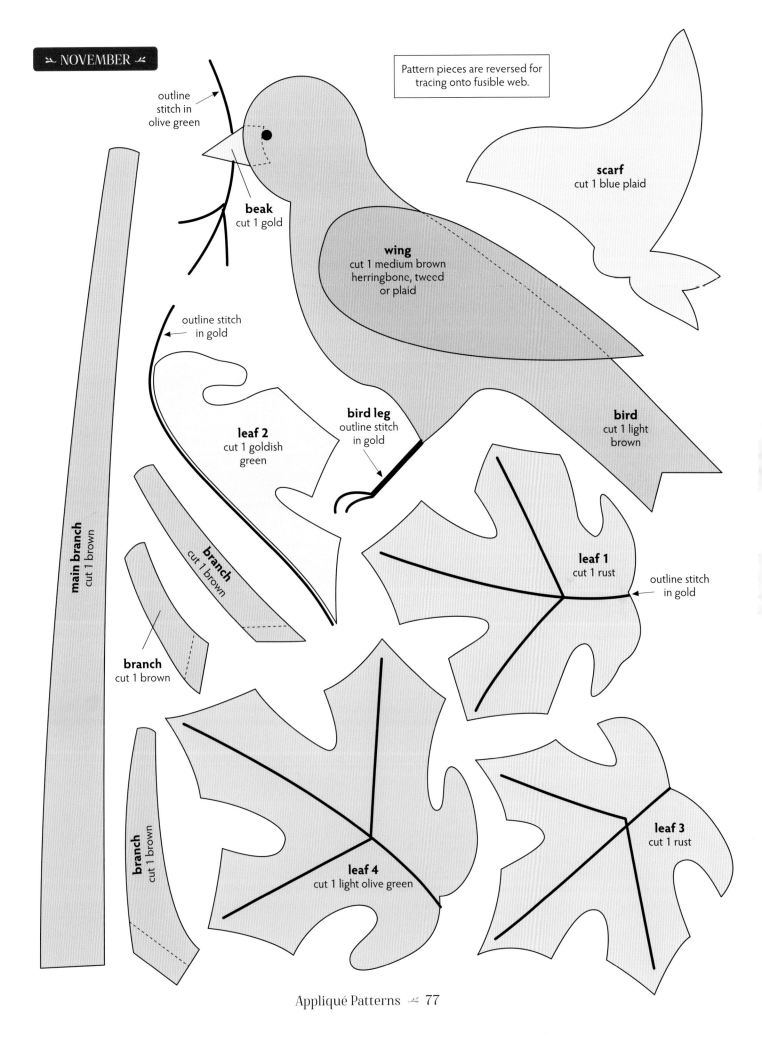

Pattern pieces are reversed for tracing onto fusible web.

outline stitch in olive green

scarf
cut 1 blue plaid

beak
cut 1 gold

wing
cut 1 medium brown
herringbone, tweed
or plaid

outline stitch
in gold

leaf 2
cut 1 goldish
green

bird leg
outline stitch
in gold

bird
cut 1 light
brown

branch
cut 1 brown

main branch
cut 1 brown

leaf 1
cut 1 rust

outline stitch
in gold

branch
cut 1 brown

branch
cut 1 brown

leaf 4
cut 1 light olive green

leaf 3
cut 1 rust

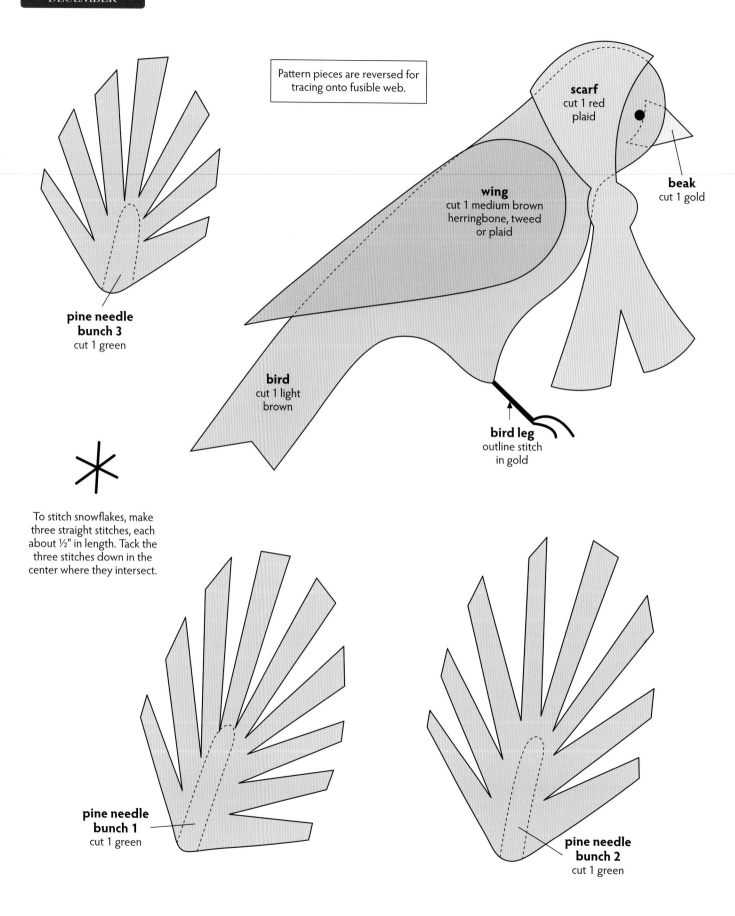

Pattern pieces are reversed for tracing onto fusible web.

**scarf**
cut 1 red plaid

**beak**
cut 1 gold

**wing**
cut 1 medium brown herringbone, tweed or plaid

**bird**
cut 1 light brown

**bird leg**
outline stitch in gold

**pine needle bunch 3**
cut 1 green

To stitch snowflakes, make three straight stitches, each about ½" in length. Tack the three stitches down in the center where they intersect.

**pine needle bunch 1**
cut 1 green

**pine needle bunch 2**
cut 1 green

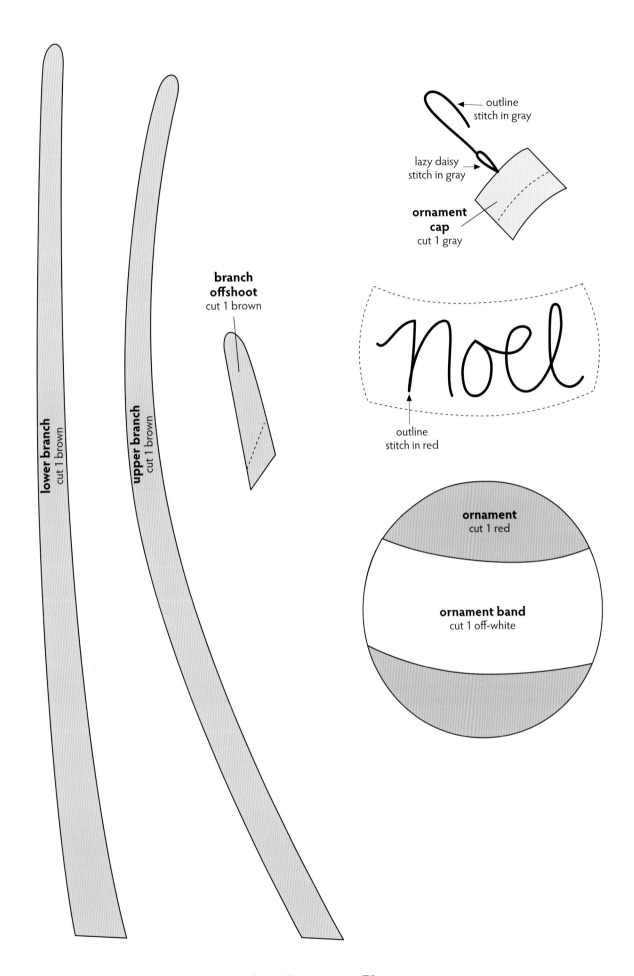

outline
stitch in gray

lazy daisy
stitch in gray

**ornament
cap**
cut 1 gray

**branch
offshoot**
cut 1 brown

*noel*

outline
stitch in red

**lower branch**
cut 1 brown

**upper branch**
cut 1 brown

**ornament**
cut 1 red

**ornament band**
cut 1 off-white

# About the Author

For as long as I can remember, I've always loved textiles; I still have remnants of my childhood blanket. My neighbor taught me how to embroider when I was seven. My mother taught 4-H sewing, and I spent many childhood hours making troll and Barbie doll clothes. I remember being fascinated by the quilts my grandmother and mother pieced and hand quilted. There is just something comforting about working with fabrics and wools, and the textures and colors have captivated me from a very young age. I never thought I'd be designing and creating for a living, but I'm thankful every day for the opportunity.

I was introduced to working with wool in 2000 and was immediately hooked. After designing several penny-rug patterns, I thought I would try my luck at the International Quilt Market and attended my first show as a vendor in May of 2002. My business quickly grew and in 2003, I began designing fabric for Maywood Studio. Because I love working with wool, I designed a line of flannels called Woolies to look like wool. The Woolies line has gone through many transformations over the years, adding new colors and textures. I love combining the Woolies flannels with wool, and all the projects in this book are made with a combination of the two. Please visit my website at AllThroughtheNight.net.